CONSUMER CHEMISTRY
PROJECTS FOR YOUNG SCIENTISTS

DAVID E. NEWTON

CONSUMER CHEMISTRY PROJECTS FOR YOUNG SCIENTISTS

PROJECTS FOR YOUNG SCIENTISTS
FRANKLIN WATTS
NEW YORK | LONDON | TORONTO | SYDNEY | 1991

————

In memory of Dr. Steve Risch,
respected colleague
and good friend

————

Photographs courtesy of: Jeff Greenberg: pp. 11, 39; Yoav/Phototake:
p. 15; Salvatore Tocci: p. 16; Stock Boston: pp. 18 (Richard Pasley),
75 (Peter Menzel); Randy Matusow: pp. 21, 29, 53, 90; Peter Arnold Inc.:
p. 69 (Leonard Lessin); Photo Researchers, Inc.: 78 top (William Carter);
Texas Department of Agriculture: p. 78 bottom.

Library of Congress Cataloging-in-Publication Data

Newton, David E.
Consumer chemistry / David E. Newton.
p.   cm. — (Projects for young scientists)
Includes bibliographical references and index.
Summary: Suggests experiments that can demonstrate basic
principles of chemistry using household items.
ISBN 0-531-11011-7
1. Chemistry—Experiments—Juvenile literature.   2. Consumer
goods—Juvenile literature.   [I. Chemistry—Experiments.
2. Experiments.]   I. Title.   II. Series.
QD38.N481991
540—dc20   90-48499   CIP   AC

CONTENTS

A NOTE ABOUT SAFETY IN DOING CHEMISTRY PROJECTS

The projects in this book are intended to be done in a science laboratory under the supervision of a qualified science teacher. Under no circumstances should you work on your own without such an adult present to approve and supervise your work.

1

CONSUMER CHEMISTRY

Ingredients: WATER, AMMONIUM LAURYL SULFATE, SODIUM LAURYL SULFATE, COCAMIDE DEA, AMMONIUM CHLORIDE, FRAGRANCE, TETRASODIUM EDTA, HONEY, BENZOPHENONE-4, WHEAT GERM OIL, CITRIC ACID, METHYLCHLOROISOTHIAZOLINONE, METHYLISOTHIAZOLINONE, DMDM HYDANTOIN, D&C ORANGE NO. 4, D&C RED NO. 33.

Does the above label look familiar? You can probably find a similar one on one of the shampoo containers in your bathroom. Today we live in a world in which unfamiliar chemicals can be found in nearly every product we buy.

What exactly are these chemicals? What function do they serve? Are they safe or harmful? Are all these chemicals necessary to clean your hair? Would soap or just plain water work just as well? Questions like these may have occurred to you before. This book is intended to help you answer such questions about the chemicals that appear in items you see and use every day.

Some of the projects given here have detailed instructions. You will be told exactly how much of each chemical to use, how long to heat a reaction, and exactly what changes to look for. In other projects, you will have to make some decisions yourself. The directions will be more in the form of hints, suggestions, and ideas. Finally, in many cases the book will do no more than raise questions, pose problems, and suggest ideas. In these instances you will really be designing your own projects, developing your own research plans, and carrying out your own instructions.

WHY DO PROJECTS?

The projects in this book may be of interest to you for one of two reasons. First, you may simply want to know more about consumer products. Second, you may be looking for an idea for a school project. In many schools today, students are expected to do original science research that can be entered in a science fair. Or they may have to do a class science project. You should be able to find some interesting ideas for such projects in this book.

Keep in mind a few ideas about school projects. First, start on your project early. Nothing spoils a project more than having to rush in order to finish your research on time. Second, be very clear as to what your project is about. State the question you want to solve and carefully outline the steps by which you will answer that question. Third, keep careful notes about your research. Buy a notebook in which you can keep a record of all your laboratory work (see Figure 1). You should have your teacher initial your book for each project to show that you have read and understood all safety precautions for that project.

Finally, find an interesting way to display your project. You have chosen a topic in which many people are interested: consumer products. Design a display that will take

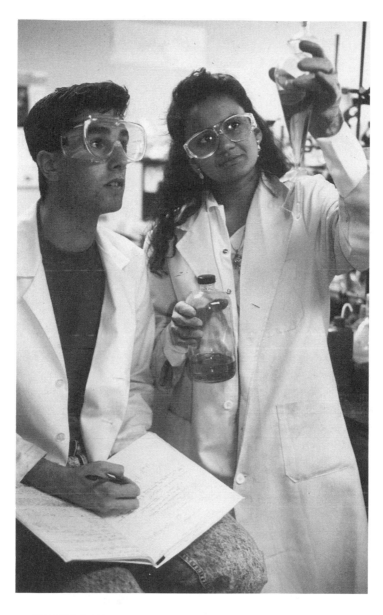

FIGURE 1. TAKING CAREFUL NOTES IS AN IMPORTANT
PART OF DOING A SCIENCE PROJECT.

advantage of that interest. Show how your project is related to a person's everyday life. State as clearly and briefly as possible what you did and what you found out in your research.

DESIGNING YOUR OWN
PROJECTS

The more experiments you do, the more skilled you will become at designing and carrying out original research. A few general suggestions at the outset, however, will help you decide how to do an original research project.

First, make sure that you work closely with a science teacher in designing your own projects. Discuss your ideas with the teacher and have that person read and approve your final plan. Be certain that you understand all the precautions you need to take to conduct the research safely.

Second, always have a clear idea as to what it is you want to find out in a research project. This book might suggest, for example, that you "find out more about the composition of face powder." Those directions are all right as a hint to the reader, but you need to rephrase that hint in much more specific terms for it to become a research topic. You might decide, for example, that you want to calculate the percentage of cornstarch in Brand X face powder. This kind of statement gives you a clear idea of exactly what it is you want to learn about this topic.

Third, you will often need to begin an experiment with some known information: a control, benchmark, or standard. For example, you may want to find out how various fertilizers affect plant growth. In order to answer that question, you have to know how a plant grows *without* fertilizer. In your project, then, you will need to grow some plants without fertilizers as well as other plants with various kinds of fertilizer. Then you can compare the effect of fertilizer against the controls, those grown without fertilizer.

Fourth, try to keep your research simple by testing no

more than one factor at a time. Maybe you have decided that you want to find out how minerals and moisture in the soil affect plant growth. You should design an experiment that tests the effect of just one of these factors at a time.

For example, in an experiment intended to show how the presence of nitrogen in the soil affects plant growth, don't worry about the effect of phosphorus, potassium, calcium, or other minerals or the effect of various amounts of moisture. You can study additional factors in later experiments. Don't be too eager to find out everything about a topic in a single experiment.

Fifth, whenever possible, try to get quantitative results in an experiment. The term *quantitative* means "numerical." Answers such as 5 g, 30 mL, 85°C, and 45% are quantitative answers. Quantitative answers always give you more detailed, more specific information about a topic than do qualitative answers such as "some," "red," "thin," "light," and "hot."

Many good books on doing original research are available. For futher information and suggestions on this topic, see the bibliography.

SAFETY

Any science project can be dangerous. Your number one responsibility in any project is knowing what might go wrong and how to prevent that from happening. Each section of this book begins with some safety notes about the projects that follow. Make sure you know the proper safety procedures for every project you work on. Discuss those procedures with your teacher before beginning. Your teacher may decide that the project is too dangerous for you to try. In that case, find another project to do.

In addition, you should learn certain general rules for working safely in a chemistry laboratory. Here are some of those rules.

1. Always work in the presence of a chemistry teacher or of a science teacher with a good knowledge of chemistry. Professional scientists don't work alone. Neither should you.

2. Always wear safety goggles when working with chemicals and chemical equipment. Figure 2 shows a common type of safety goggles recommended for use in science labs. Since you never know when something will go wrong, you do not have time to run and get your eye protection if and when you actually need it. Have your teacher inspect and approve the goggles you use. Avoid wearing contact lenses in the lab.

3. Always wear a lab coat, lab apron, or other protective clothing, as shown in Figure 2. Spilling acid on a new shirt is not as tragic as getting acid in your eye. But why lose the shirt? A lab coat or lab apron will protect you from this kind of accident.

4. Always assume that a chemical is poisonous and dangerous unless you absolutely know differently. That means:
   a. *Never taste a chemical.*
   b. *Never smell a chemical unless your teacher allows you to do so.* Then you can check the odor by waving your hand over the top of the chemical, bringing a small amount of the odor to your nose. Figure 3 shows the proper way of testing the odor of a chemical.
   c. *Treat all chemicals as if they were highly corrosive, as if they will burn your skin, dissolve your clothes, or have other harmful effects.* That means:
      1. Don't get chemicals on your skin.
      2. Wipe chemicals up when they are spilled.
      3. Do not eat or drink while you are doing experiments.

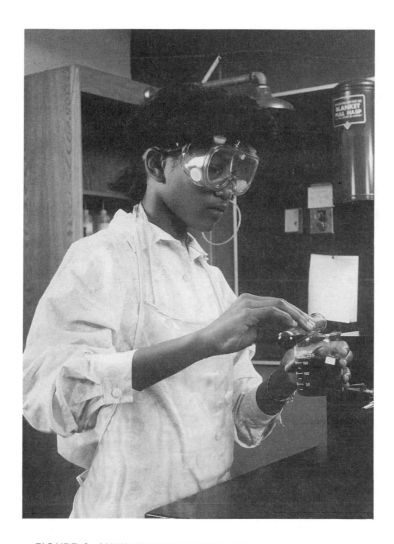

FIGURE 2. ALWAYS WEAR SAFETY GOGGLES AND A LAB
APRON OR LAB COAT WHEN WORKING IN THE LAB.
ALSO BE SURE TO HAVE SAFETY EQUIPMENT
(LIKE THE SAFETY BLANKET AND SAFETY
SHOWER BEHIND THE STUDENT) AVAILABLE AND
TO KNOW WHERE IT IS LOCATED IN YOUR
CLASSROOM AND HOW TO USE IT.

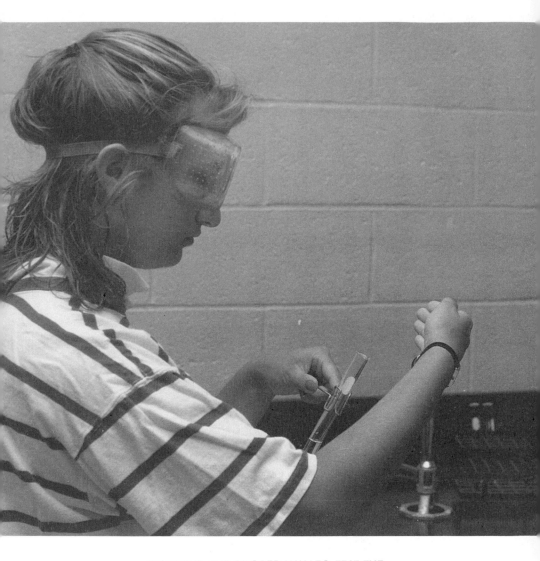

FIGURE 3. THE PROPER WAY TO TEST THE
ODOR OF A CHEMICAL IS TO GENTLY WAVE YOUR
HAND OVER THE TOP OF THE TEST TUBE.
NEVER STICK YOUR NOSE OVER THE TOP
OF THE TUBE AND SNIFF DIRECTLY.

d. *Never handle any chemical with your hands.* Always use a spatula or some other tool to pick up a chemical. If the chemical touches your skin, wash immediately with soap and water.

5. Use special care when heating any object. Normally you will use a Bunsen or alcohol burner to heat containers. Have your teacher demonstrate the correct method for using these burners. Never look into a container that is being heated. Never point the mouth of the container that is being heated at anyone else. Figure 4 shows how to heat a test tube.

a. If you have long hair, be sure to restrain it or arrange it so it will stay out of flames.

6. Become familiar with the safety equipment in your laboratory and know how to implement first-aid and emergency procedures. Have your teacher show you where the eyeshower, safety shower, fire extinguisher, and fire blanket are located and how they are used. Know how to operate such equipment and have the assurance of your teacher that the items work properly. Make sure the safety equipment is immediately accessible to your work space. Figure 2 shows a fire blanket and a safety shower.

7. Do not dispose of chemicals down the drain or into the trash. Have your teacher explain how chemical wastes are handled in your school. Ask your teacher how to dispose of other materials and equipment.

8. Wash your hands after you finish conducting an experiment.

9. Always keep your work area neat and clean, as shown in the prior figures. A messy work space can cause serious accidents.

FIGURE 4. THE CORRECT WAY TO HEAT A TEST
TUBE OVER A BURNER. NEVER POINT THE TUBE
TOWARD YOURSELF OR TOWARD ANYONE ELSE.

10. Make sure that you understand the safety precautions for every project you work on. At the beginning of each project in this book is a set of safety notes. These notes list the precautions you must observe in your work. Learn the meanings of the following terms used in the safety notes:

   a. **caustic**—any material that will burn or destroy tissue is termed *caustic*. The term normally refers to the class of chemicals called bases (see the glossary for the definition of *base*).

   b. **corrosive**—any material that irritates, burns, or destroys tissue is termed *corrosive*. The term often refers to the class of chemicals called acids (see the glossary for the definition of *acid*).

   c. **flammable**—any material that will catch fire or burn easily is termed *flammable*.

   d. **irritant**—any material that makes the skin, eyes, or nose sore or sensitive is termed an *irritant*.

   e. **toxic**—any material that is poisonous is termed *toxic*.

11. Additional information on the safety of chemicals, on first-aid procedures, and on the disposal of chemicals can be found in the books listed in the bibliography in the section on laboratory safety.

12. Ask your teacher to go over the safety notes with you and to initial your laboratory notebook to show that you have read and understood the safety notes.

Your teacher may want to review other safety procedures with you. Have him or her read the above list. Then find out what other safety rules you need to follow in working in this teacher's laboratory.

Now you are ready to begin your research on the role of chemistry in consumer products.

2

FOODS

What would life be like without food? The smells, tastes, colors, and textures of food provide a thousand delights, and mealtimes are often social occasions, from simple family gatherings to august ceremonial events. In most cultures, the act of eating even has important religious significance. Figure 5 shows an array of different foods.

But the answer to the question at the beginning of this chapter is more basic than any of the above reasons for eating. Most important, food provides us with nutrients, the substances our bodies need to stay alive, to grow, and to develop. In this chapter you will see how to test for some major components that make up foods.

The components of foods can be classified into a few major groups, including carbohydrates, fats, proteins, vitamins and minerals, fiber, and water. Each of these components has one or more important functions in the body. For example, carbohydrates and fats provide the energy that our bodies need in order to stay alive, to move around, and to grow.

FIGURE 5. VARIETY IS THE SPICE OF LIFE.

Proteins provide the body with compounds from which it makes new body parts: skin, muscle, nerves, and other tissue. Vitamins and minerals make possible the thousands of chemical reactions that take place in a normal, healthy body every second.

The foods you eat today differ greatly from those your grandparents ate. A large fraction of today's foods are processed—cooked, canned, dried, frozen, irradiated, and treated with chemicals—before you buy them. That means the foods you eat contain many food additives, materials that do not occur naturally in the products you buy. You also will do some research on food additives in this chapter.

SOURCES OF ENERGY

The energy a food supplies your body is measured in Calories. A Calorie is the amount of heat needed to raise the temperature of 1 kg of water 1°C. In research laboratories, food is burned the way coal is burned in a furnace. The heat from the burning food warms a container of water. By measuring the increase in temperature of the water, a scientist can find out how many Calories the food contains.

SAFETY NOTES
1. Review the general safety precautions on pages 14–19.
2. Wear safety goggles and a lab apron.
3. Use caution with flames.

You can do a simplified version of this experiment. Figure 6 shows the equipment you will use. What you need to think about is the idea behind the experiment. You set fire to the food item as shown in the diagram. As the food burns, it warms the water in the container. You take the

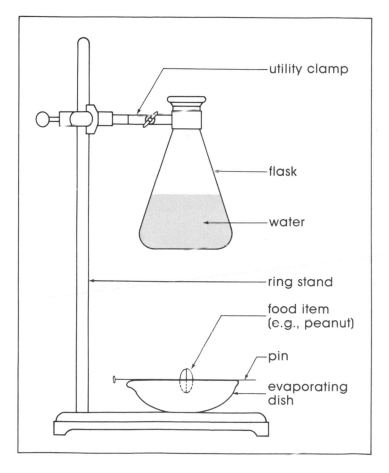

FIGURE 6. THE EQUIPMENT USED IN FINDING
THE NUMBER OF CALORIES IN FOODS

temperature of the water before the food is ignited and again after it has burned completely.

You also need to know the weight of the water and the food. Use a laboratory balance to determine the weight of each item as exactly as possible. You can calculate the number of Calories in the food by the following formula:

$$\begin{array}{l}\text{number of}\\\text{Calories}\\\text{(per gram}\\\text{of food)}\end{array} = \dfrac{\begin{array}{c}\text{weight of water}\\\text{(in grams)}\end{array} \times \begin{array}{c}\text{increase in}\\\text{temperature}\\\text{(in °C)}\end{array}}{\begin{array}{c}\text{weight of food}\\\text{(in grams)}\end{array} \times 1,000}$$

You can use this equipment to measure the heat value of many foods. The easiest food to begin with is probably a nut of some kind, for example, a peanut or walnut. You can test other foods, too, but some will burn better than others. Remember to be careful when working with flames and keep in mind that some foods are more flammable than others (for example, those containing a lot of fat).

You probably should repeat the experiment a few times with each food. If the results are about the same two or three times in a row, the experiment is going well. If you get very different results, you probably are making a mistake somewhere.

Another challenge in this experiment is to reduce the number of possible errors. For example, you would like to have *all* the heat produced by the burning food captured by the water. But that is difficult. Some heat will escape into the surrounding air. What changes can you make in the equipment to reduce this error?

As you do the experiment the first time, look for other sources of error. See if you can find ways to reduce each error you discover.

SUGARS

An important source of Calories in your diet is carbohydrates. Sugars are one kind of carbohydrate. You can detect the presence of sugars in foods with some simple chemical tests.

SAFETY NOTES
1.   Review the general safety precautions on pages 14–19.
2.   Wear safety goggles and a lab apron.
3.   Benedict's solution is toxic. If you spill any on yourself, wash it off immediately with soap and water.

Before you begin, obtain the following items.

1.   Benedict's solution (at least 100 mL)

2.   glucose (grape sugar, corn sugar)

3.   fructose (fruit sugar)

4.   sucrose (table sugar)

5.   any other sugars you can find (try a natural foods store or ask your chemistry teacher).

Make a solution of each sugar by dissolving 1 g of the sugar in 10 mL of water. Add 5 mL of Benedict's solution to a test tube and heat the solution slowly just to boiling, over a Bunsen burner or alcohol burner. When you see bubbles forming in the solution, the solution will be close to boiling. *Carefully* add 5 drops of the glucose solution to the hot Benedict's solution. Keep the solution warm for about 30 seconds. Make a note of any changes you see.

Empty the test tube, wash it out well, and add another 5 mL of Benedict's solution. Repeat the testing process with each of your sugar solutions, one at a time. Do not heat any of the solution longer than about 30 seconds. Make a note of the changes you see, if any, with each solution.

What have you learned from these experiments about the use of Benedict's solution in testing for sugars?

The sugar you probably will be most interested in testing for is sucrose, the sugar in your sugar bowl at home. It is also the sugar added most often to commercial foods.

Heating a sucrose solution and boiling it for 5 minutes converts the sucrose to glucose and another sugar, fructose. A color change from blue to orange or red is a positive test for glucose.

Obtain a half-dozen foods that you want to test for sucrose. You could try some (like breakfast cereal) that you know contain sucrose. You could select other foods by looking on labels to see if sucrose is listed as an ingredient. And you could choose some foods about which you have no advance information as to the presence of sucrose.

STARCHES

Starches are also carbohydrates. They are large, complex molecules made of sugar molecules.

Starch reacts with iodine to give a dark blue complex compound. Only starch among the carbohydrates shows this reaction, so you can use iodine to test for the presence of starch in foods.

SAFETY NOTES
1. Review the general safety precautions on pages 14–19.
2. Wear safety goggles and a lab apron.
3. Solid iodine and iodine solution are toxic. You will be using an iodine solution that contains only a very small amount of iodine. If you spill any of the solution on yourself, wash it off immediately with soap and water.

Ask your teacher for a 1% iodine solution to use in this test. Add 5 drops of the iodine solution to 10 mL of water. Use this as your iodine test solution in the following experiments.

Place 5 g of dry starch on a glass plate. Put 1 drop of the iodine test solution on top of the starch. Look for a blue to dark blue spot where the iodine comes into contact with the starch.

Now try the iodine test on a starch solution. Starch does not dissolve very well in water, but you can make a starch suspension in the following way. Add about 5 mL of water to 1 g of starch in an evaporating dish. Add the water slowly, using a spatula to rub it into the starch until you have a smooth paste. Then add this starch paste to 100 mL of boiling water slowly and with constant stirring. You should end up with a milky suspension without any lumps in it. Test 5 mL of this starch solution with 1 drop of the iodine test solution.

Now that you have learned how to test for starch, use this test to determine whether starch is present in various foods. Select some raw materials (such as a potato), some grains (such as flour), some processed foods (such as cereal), and any other food that you think might contain starch. You will have to think about a way of preparing each food for the iodine test. You can, for example, just slice a piece of potato and drop the iodine test solution on it. But how will you test for starch in, say, a spoonful of rice flour?

You might also think about ways of making this test quantitative. That is, how would you go about comparing the amount of starch in various foods?

FATS AND OILS

Fats and oils have many functions in your body. They are an important source of energy. They store some vitamins and other important compounds. Fats help protect internal organs from damage and act as insulation for your body. The simplest test for fats and oils requires nothing more complicated than a brown paper bag.

SAFETY NOTES
1. Review the general safety precautions on pages 14–19.
2. Wear safety goggles and a lab apron.
3. Potassium bisulfate is toxic and is an irritant. If you spill any on yourself, wash it off immediately with soap and water.

Rub a piece of animal fat on the bag. Place a drop of vegetable oil in another spot on the bag. Place a drop of water in a third spot on the bag. Compare the three spots. Look at them an hour after they were placed on the bag and compare them again. The translucent greasy spot you see is characteristic of any material that contains a fat or oil.

Select a half-dozen products that you think may contain a fat or oil. Select three more that you think do *not* contain a fat or oil. Try the paper bag test to see if your predictions are correct. What do you think will happen with the cheese curls shown in Figure 7?

Another test for fats and oils depends on the production of a strong-smelling compound called acrolein. If you have ever burned bacon while cooking it, you may have smelled the sharp, biting odor of acrolein. Here's how to do the acrolein test.

Combine 5 drops of vegetable oil with 1 g of potassium bisulfate (potassium hydrogen sulfate) in a test tube. Warm the test tube gently for a few minutes. *Cautiously check the odor of the gas formed in this reaction. Use the procedure for smelling a gas explained on page 14, section 14b.* The gas you smell is acrolein.

INGREDIENTS: CORN MEAL VEGETA-
BLE OIL (CONTAINS ONE OR MORE
OF THE FOLLOWING OILS: COTTON-
SEED, SOYBEAN, PARTIALLY HY-
DROGENATED SOYBEAN OR PAR-
TIALLY HYDROGENATED COTTON-
SEED, CANOLA), AGED CHEDDAR
CHEESE (PASTEURIZED MILK, SALT,
CHEESE CULTURES, ENZYMES),
WHEY SOLIDS, SALT, HYDROLYZED
CEREAL SOLIDS, BLUE CHEESE
(PASTEURIZED MILK, SALT, CHEESE
CULTURES, ENZYMES), SODIUM
PHOSPHATE, MONOSODIUM GLU-
TAMATE, CITRIC ACID, SPICES,
ARTIFICIAL COLOR INCLUDING
F.D.&C. YELLOW #5 AND #6, AND
LACTIC ACID.

FIGURE 7. DO YOU THINK CHEESE CURLS
MIGHT BE A GOOD PRODUCT TO TEST FOR
THE PRESENCE OF A FAT OR OIL?

Repeat the acrolein test on three other fats and oils. Then repeat the test on some foods that you think may contain fats or oils and on some you think do not contain fats or oils. How accurate are your predictions?

PROTEINS

Thousands of different proteins exist. Some tests identify *any* kind of protein. Other tests identify only certain types of proteins. The biuret and ninhydrin tests are examples of the former, while the xanthoproteic test is an example of the latter.

SAFETY NOTES
1. Review the general safety precautions on pages 14–19.
2. Wear safety goggles and a lab apron.
3. Sodium hydroxide, whether solid or in solution, is caustic and toxic and is an irritant. It will burn your skin and dissolve clothing. If you spill any on yourself, wash it off immediately with soap and water. Copper(II) sulfate is an irritant and is toxic if swallowed. Ninhydrin is toxic and stains the skin. If you spill any of these chemicals on yourself, wash it off immediately with soap and water.

The simplest protein to use in this project is egg white. You can also make an egg-whitelike solution by dissolving 2 g of powdered egg albumin in 100 mL of water.

Biuret Test
Place 5 mL of egg white or egg albumin solution in each of two test tubes. To the first test tube *carefully* add 2 mL

of a 10% sodium hydroxide solution, which your teacher has prepared. Add 5 drops of a 1% copper(II) sulfate solution to the same test tube. A 1% copper(II) sulfate solution contains 1 g of copper(II) sulfate dissolved in 100 mL of water. Stir the mixture thoroughly. The color change you see is characteristic of any protein.

Ninhydrin Test
Another test that works with almost any protein is the ninhydrin test. Ask your teacher for a small amount of ninhydrin reagent. Add 1 mL of this reagent to the second test tube of egg white or egg albumin solution. The blue-violet color you see is characteristic of nearly any protein.

Testing Foods
Select a number of foods that you think *do* contain protein and some that you think *do not* contain protein. Using the biuret or ninhydrin test, see if your predictions about these foods are correct. Of those that test positive for protein, find out which ones have protein that contains the benzene ring.

VITAMIN C

The tests for most vitamins are too difficult for you to do. But the tests for vitamin C are exceptions. Vitamin C is the vitamin found in oranges, lemons, limes, and other citrus fruits. It prevents scurvy and increases the body's resistance to infections.

Two simple tests can be used to determine the presence and amount of vitamin C in foods. The first test makes use of the *indicator* known as indophenol. An indicator is a dye that is one color in one solution and a second color in another. If you can't find indophenol, try the second method described on page 33, which uses the starch–iodine test.

Indophenol Method

Crush and dissolve a 50-mg vitamin C tablet in 100 mL of water. This solution will provide you with a standard against which you can compare other solutions. You know how much vitamin C is in this standard solution: 50 mg.

Add indophenol solution drop by drop to the vitamin C solution. Swirl the flask as you add the indophenol. As the indophenol reacts with vitamin C, it changes from dark blue to pale pink or colorless. Watch for the point at which a single drop of indophenol retains its blue color. At this point, all the vitamin C in the solution has been used up (has reacted). Record the number of drops needed to react with 50 mg of vitamin C.

Select a number of foods that you know or believe to contain vitamin C. Among those to try are orange juice, apple juice, grapefruit juice, tomato juice, and artificial fruit juices. You may want to compare fresh fruit juices with frozen and canned juices for vitamin C content. Include some fresh fruits and vegetables in your tests. In this case, decide how you can get the fruit or vegetable into a form in which it can be tested by the above procedure.

Use the indophenol test to determine the amount of vitamin C in each food product. Express your answer as a weight percentage. You can calculate the weight percentage by the following formula:

$$\frac{\text{weight}}{\text{percentage}} = \frac{\text{mg of vitamin C}}{\text{g of food tested} \times 1{,}000} \times 100\%$$

You can find the amount of vitamin C in the sample by comparing the number of drops of indophenol needed in the test sample ("y drops" in the formula below) compared to the number of drops needed for the standard sample ("x drops" in the formula below). The calculation is as follows:

$$\frac{y \text{ drops}}{? \text{ mg vitamin C}} = \frac{x \text{ drops}}{50 \text{ mg vitamin C}}$$

You can solve this proportion by cross-multiplying:

$$? \text{ mg vitamin C} = \frac{y \text{ drops} \times 50 \text{ mg vitamin C}}{x \text{ drops}}$$

Some foods may be inexpensive but contain little vitamin C. Others may be more costly but may be rich in vitamin C. Find a way to calculate the amount of vitamin C per penny you can get from the foods you test.

Starch—Iodine Test

SAFETY NOTES
1. Review the general safety precautions on pages 14–19.
2. Wear safety goggles and a lab apron.
3. Solid iodine and iodine solution are toxic. You will be using an iodine solution that contains only a very small amount of iodine. If you spill any of the solution on yourself, wash it off immediately with soap and water.

Make 100 mL of standard vitamin C solution with a vitamin C tablet, as instructed in the indophenol test. To 100 mL of this solution add 1 mL of starch solution. (See page 27 for instructions on making a starch solution.) Then add a 1% iodine solution, dispensed by your teacher, to the vitamin C/starch mixture drop by drop.

As long as vitamin C is present, the iodine you add will react with it. As soon as the vitamin C is all gone, the next drop of iodine will react with starch, forming the characteristic dark blue with which you are familiar. Count the number of drops of iodine solution needed to react with 50 mg of vitamin C. Then continue your tests on other foods, as described above, using starch and iodine in place of indophenol.

Effects of Cooking and Chemicals on Vitamin C

Vitamin C is rather easily lost from foods. For one thing, it dissolves in water. Also, the vitamin C molecule is somewhat fragile. It is destroyed by heat and by certain chemicals. Foods that are cooked or processed, therefore, tend to lose some of their vitamin C.

SAFETY NOTES
1. Review the general safety precautions on pages 14–19.
2. Wear safety goggles and a lab apron.

Find out what effect cooking has on the amount of vitamin C in food. To do so, measure the amount of vitamin C in a sample of food. Then cook the food for a period of time. Finally, measure the amount of vitamin C in the cooked food.

You will need to find a way to do this. One possibility is to measure the amount of vitamin C in the raw and cooked foods. Another way is to measure the amount of vitamin C that remains in the water used to cook the food you test. What would this tell you?

Your task is complicated by the fact that food loses vitamin C for two reasons. Some of the vitamin C simply dissolves and can later be found in the cooking water. But some of the vitamin C is actually changed chemically into another substance and cannot be detected in the cooking water. Figure out a way to separate these two effects.

You also may want to investigate how cooking *time* affects the loss of vitamin C, if at all. That is, does it make any difference if you cook something for 1 minute, 5 minutes, or 10 minutes in terms of the amount of vitamin C lost? Devise a method for answering this question.

Sodium bicarbonate (baking soda) is sometimes added to foods cooked at home or processed commercially. Devise a method for finding out how sodium bicarbonate affects the vitamin C content of foods. Make sure that you separate out other effects such as damage by heating and solubility of water, tested for above.

IRON

The tests for most minerals are very difficult, but here is one test for iron. Your body uses iron to make the red blood cells that carry oxygen from your lungs to the cells.

SAFETY NOTES
1. Review the general safety precautions on pages 14–19.
2. Wear safety goggles and a lab apron.
3. Potassium thiocyanate is toxic. If you spill any on yourself, wash it off immediately with soap and water.
4. Nitric acid is corrosive and toxic and is an irritant. Use caution in working with nitric acid. If you spill any on yourself, wash it off immediately with soap and water.

The mineral iron occurs in many foods. Liver and other red meats are rich sources. Iron is also added to many foods processed commercially.

Try your first test for iron on an iron supplement pill or a "multivitamin" pill that also contains iron. Read the label to see how much is in the pill you test.

Crush the pill and dissolve it in 50 mL of water. Add 5 drops of dilute nitric acid and 1 mL of a 0.1 M solution of potassium thiocyanate, dispensed by your teacher. A 0.1 M solution of potassium thiocyanate is made by dissolving 1 g of solid potassium thiocyanate in 100 mL of *distilled water*, a process your teacher should do. The red color you see when potassium thiocyanate is added to the vitamin pill is iron(III) thiocyanate, a clear test for the presence of iron in a material.

Now select a food to test for iron. Some good sources include fish, eggs, green vegetables, beans and peas, and whole grain cereals. The easiest food with which to begin might be plain dry cereal, one with no nuts, fruits, or other "extras" in it. Put 5 g of the cereal in an evaporating dish, grind it to a powder, and heat it until it has turned completely to ash.

Wash the ash from the evaporating dish into a beaker and dilute to a volume of 50 mL. Stir the solution well and filter. To the *filtrate* add 5 drops of dilute nitric acid and 1 mL of a 0.1 M solution of potassium thiocyanate. Look for the characteristic red color of iron(III) thiocyanate. Test for iron in some of the other foods mentioned in the preceding paragraph. Refer to the appendix for more information on the technique of *filtration.*

Think of a way to estimate the amount of iron in a food. Do some of the sources listed above contain more iron than others? Start with your "vitamin pill" standard. That standard tells you that x mg of iron (listed on the label) in 50 mL of solution produces a red color of a certain intensity with potassium thiocyanate. Make another solution using the same vitamin pill and twice as much water. See how intense the red color is this time. Now you know that x mg/2 of iron (a solution half as concentrated as the first one) produces a red color of another intensity with potassium thiocyanate.

You can make further dilutions to measure the color intensity of x mg/4, x mg/8, x mg/16, etc., on solutions of iron. If you line up these solutions in a row of test tubes, you will have a set of standards against which to compare your tests of iron in various foods. Try to estimate the relative amount of iron in some of the foods mentioned above.

3

DETERGENTS

The term *detergent* refers to any material used for cleaning. Probably the first detergent to be discovered was soap. The process for making soap is one of the first chemical processes discovered by humans. Long before the science of chemistry had begun, men and women were making soap in their own homes. One reason that soap making was discovered so early may be that the materials required for this process are so readily available. All a person needs is a fat or oil, ashes, and boiling water. Ashes contain a chemical—lye—that converts the fat or oil to soap. Ashes are seldom used in soap making today. Figure 8 shows the commercial soap-making process.

MAKING SOAP

You can make your own soap in pretty much the way it has always been made.

FIGURE 8. THE PROCESS FOR MAKING
SOAP WAS ONE OF THE FIRST CHEMICAL
PROCESSES DISCOVERED BY HUMANS.

Be sure to work under supervision in this project. Work behind a shield if possible.

For your first experience with soap-making you will need about 15 mL of an oil (cottonseed oil works well), an equal volume of ethyl alcohol (ethanol), and 5 mL of a 40% solution of lye. Lye is sodium hydroxide. Ask your teacher to prepare a 40% solution of lye for you.

Combine the oil, alcohol, and lye solution in a large evaporating dish. Cover the evaporating dish loosely with a glass plate. Heat the evaporating dish on a steam bath, as shown in Figure 9 and in the appendix under "4. Water Baths." Stir the mixture from time to time. *Use care* when you remove the glass plate to stir, as the solution tends to spatter. Make sure you are wearing safety goggles. After about 30 minutes, you should see the soap beginning to form in the evaporating dish.

Allow the evaporating dish to cool. Then transfer the mixture from the evaporating dish into the beaker on which it has been sitting. Heat the beaker until the mixture is very hot, but not boiling. The hot water in the beaker will dissolve any lye that did not react with the oil. You want to remove the excess lye since sodium hydroxide is a very caustic material. Any lye left in the soap will produce a

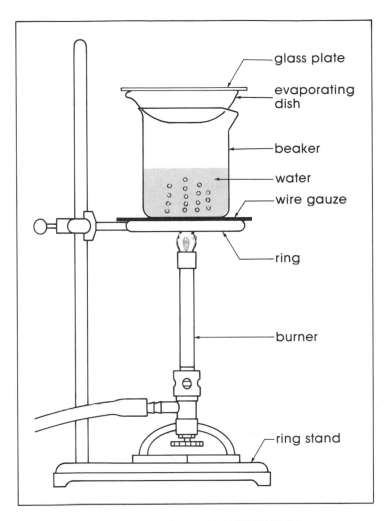

FIGURE 9. THE STEAM BATH USED IN
THE SOAP-MAKING PROJECT

harsh product that will irritate your skin when you use the soap.

Allow the solution in the beaker to cool for about 5 minutes. Then add 50 mL of a saturated solution of sodium chloride to the beaker. You can make a saturated solution of sodium chloride by dissolving 18 g of sodium chloride in 50 mL of water.

The sodium chloride solution will cause the soap to precipitate out of solution. Wear plastic or rubber gloves for the next step. The gloves will protect your hands from any lye remaining in the soap. Pour off the liquid in the beaker and collect the solid pieces of soap that remain. You may be able to squeeze these pieces together into a single lump. Wash the soap several times with cold water and press it dry in paper towels.

Your homemade soap will probably look and smell different from the soap you buy in stores. But chemically, your soap and commercial soap are quite similar and should work about equally well as cleansers. Save your homemade soap for testing in the section on "Testing Soaps."

Variations on the Process
The two main components of your homemade soap are oil and lye. You can try varying each of these components. For example, you might see what differences you can achieve by using other kinds of oils, for example, corn oil, olive oil, peanut oil, and safflower oil. How are the appearance, odor, sudsing ability, and other properties of soap affected by using other oils? Save the soaps you make for these tests to use in the "Testing Soaps" section later in this chapter.

You can also use fats instead of oils. Our ancestors made soap using the fat from cows, pigs, and other animals slaughtered for food. Collect fat trimmed from steaks, chops, and other pieces of meat by the cook in your house, or ask your local butcher for some small pieces of waste fat. How does soap made from pork fat differ from soap made from beef fat? How do "fat" soaps differ from "oil" soaps?

Finally, you can try using cooking fats like lard or Crisco

instead of an oil. Find out whether soaps made with these starting materials differ from your original homemade soap.

You also can substitute other chemicals for the lye used in making your soap. Lye is used to make soap because sodium hydroxide—lye—contains the hydroxide group. The hydroxide is the "working part" of the lye molecule in this reaction. Other compounds that contain the hydroxide group can be substituted for lye, for example, potassium hydroxide. *Keep in mind that potassium hydroxide, like lye, is very caustic. Be sure to work under supervision and to follow the same safety procedures when working with potassium hydroxide as you would with lye.*

Find out how the potassium soap(s) you make differ from the sodium soap(s) you made.

CHANGING THE
APPEARANCE OF SOAP

The soap you buy at a store has an attractive shape, color, and odor. You can treat your homemade soap to accomplish similar effects.

For example, you can add coloring to your soap. The easiest way to do that is to add a small piece of wax crayon to the soap while it is still liquid. The crayon dissolves in the soap and gives it color. The soap will not be exactly the same color as the crayon, however, and you may have to make a few trials to get exactly the color you want.

A few drops of perfume will add odor to your soap. Again, add the perfume while the soap is still liquid. Stir in the perfume well so that it mixes completely with the soap. Use only a small amount of perfume, as a little of it goes a long way!

Some commercial soaps also contain cold cream. What advantage would this kind of soap have over regular hand soap? You can add cold cream to your homemade soap, too. At the point at which your soap is still soft, add up to one-third the volume of cold cream to the soap. Blend the mixture thoroughly before allowing it to cool.

Do any of these characteristics affect the ability of soap to get things clean? Design a project that will allow you to answer this question.

MAKING A
SYNTHETIC DETERGENT

Just as you can make your own soap so, too, can you make your own detergent, although synthetic detergents (also called *syndets*) are more difficult to make than soaps. **Carry out the following project only under the close supervision of a qualified science teacher and try to work behind a shield.**

SAFETY NOTES
1. Review the general safety precautions on pages 14–19.
2. Wear safety goggles, gloves, and a lab apron.
3. Lauryl alcohol is flammable. Keep it away from flames.
4. Concentrated sulfuric acid is very corrosive. It will burn your skin and dissolve clothing. If you spill any on yourself, wash it off immediately with soap and water.
5. Lye (sodium hydroxide), whether solid or in solution is caustic and toxic and is an irritant. It will burn your skin and dissolve clothing. If you spill any on yourself, wash it off immediately with soap and water.
6. A large amount of heat is released when sodium hydroxide or concentrated sulfuric acid is added to water or alcohol. Always add the lye or the acid slowly and cautiously while stirring. Watch out for spattering.

Place 25 g of lauryl alcohol in a beaker. *Slowly and cautiously* add 10 mL of concentrated sulfuric acid to the alcohol. In a second beaker, have your teacher dissolve 4 g of sodium hydroxide in 50 mL of water.

Finally, add the contents of the first beaker (lauryl alcohol and sulfuric acid) to the second beaker *slowly* and with constant stirring. The white solid formed within the solution as the result of a chemical reaction—the precipitate—is sodium lauryl sulfate. Many syndets contain this or a related compound as their main ingredient.

Filter the white precipitate with a Büchner funnel if possible. (Ask your teacher to show you how to use the Büchner funnel.) Finally, set the precipitate aside until it is thoroughly dry. You can use this detergent in the tests of soaps and detergents that follow.

TESTING SOAPS
AND DETERGENTS

What makes a good soap? One measure of soap quality is how easily the soap makes suds. For example, you might find a soap on sale at your local store for 59 cents a bar. In comparison, your regular soap might sell for 89 cents a bar. But what if you have to use twice as much of the bargain soap to make the same amount of suds as you get from your regular soap? Is the bargain soap really a bargain then? Here's a way to test the suds-making ability of your soaps.

SAFETY NOTES
1. Review the general safety precautions on pages 14–19.
2. Wear safety goggles and a lab apron.

Start with a liquid soap since that's the easiest form in which to test soaps. Add one drop of the liquid soap to 10 mL of distilled water in a test tube. Stopper the test tube and shake it for five seconds. See if suds form and last for 10 seconds. If not, add another drop of soap and repeat the process.

What you are trying to do is to find the number of drops of soap needed to get suds that last for 10 seconds. Write down the number of drops required for "permanent" sudsing (suds that last at least 10 seconds) with your first sample of soap.

Now repeat this procedure with other soaps. Collect as many commercial liquid soaps as you can find. Write down the cost per ounce of each soap you collect. Test each one to see how many drops are needed to form "permanent" suds (suds that last at least 10 seconds). Figure out a way to calculate the value of each soap. One way to compare soap value is to find the sudsing ability per penny of cost for the soap.

You can use this same procedure to test detergents. Collect a variety of liquid detergents and conduct the "sudsing" test on them. How do detergents compare to liquid soaps on the sudsing test? How do they compare on the basis of their cost?

Soaps and detergents come in forms other than liquid, of course. For example, the soaps you made earlier are solids. The best way to test solid soaps and detergents is to make them first into liquids. Then you can use the procedure described above to test their sudsing ability.

Remember that solid soaps tend to melt rather easily. Find a way of melting solid soaps in warm water for the sudsing tests. Remember to use exactly the same amount of each kind of soap. How do you think you could test powdered cleaning agents like laundry soaps and detergents with the same sudsing test?

At the conclusion of these experiments, prepare a "Sudsing Ability" chart and a "Detergent Value" chart. The first chart should compare the sudsing effectiveness of the detergents you studied. The second chart should include the price factor in comparing your products.

• The ability to make suds is not the only test for soaps

and detergents. Some cleaning agents are made so as *not* to make a lot of suds. Where and why in your house would you use a low-sudsing detergent?

• Another way to test a cleaning agent is to see how clean it gets a piece of dirty cloth. Get an old piece of sheet and make it dirty with mud. Make sure the sheet is equally muddy everywhere. Let the sheet dry before cutting it into 3-cm squares. Collect as many soaps and detergents as possible to test. Add a square of dirty cloth and the same amount (weight) of each detergent to a test tube. Shake the test tubes well for about 30 seconds. Remove each cloth, rinse it, and let it dry. Place the test cloths next to each other and decide which cleaning agent worked best.

• The above procedure will not give very dependable results. It might be hard to tell just by looking which cloth is cleanest after the tests. Can you find another way of comparing the cleaning abilities of various detergents?

• Soaps and detergents should be able to remove more than simple dirt from a cloth. Invent a method for finding out how well your cleaning agents remove oil from a cloth.

• What materials other than dirt and oil should a soap or detergent remove? Test your cleaning agents on cloths soiled with some of the other materials you name.

HARDNESS IN WATER

You choose a soap or detergent because of its ability to get things clean. But other factors are involved in the cleaning process. One of the most important of these is the water you wash in. Water differs almost everywhere. The water you use for drinking, cooking, and washing may be very different from the water used by a cousin who lives only 30 miles away.

Some kinds of water are called "hard" because it is hard to make suds in them. Hard water can be either temporary or permanent. You will shortly see the difference in these two kinds of hard water.

Hard water usually contains salts of magnesium, calcium, and/or iron. Here's how to make a sample of permanent hard water and temporary hard water to use in the following projects.

SAFETY NOTES
1.   Wear safety goggles and a lab apron.
2.   Epsom salts (magnesium sulfate) are toxic.

Add 5 g of Epsom salts (magnesium sulfate) to 250 mL of distilled water in a beaker. Stir until the solid has completely dissolved. This solution is an example of permanent hard water.

Add 5 g of calcium bicarbonate to 250 mL of distilled water in a beaker. Stir vigorously for about a minute. Allow the beaker to sit for about 5 minutes. Then carefully pour off the clear solution into a second beaker. Don't let any of the undissolved calcium bicarbonate at the bottom of the first beaker get into the second beaker. The clear solution of calcium bicarbonate is an example of temporary hard water.

Now you are ready to compare the hardness of various water samples. Select any commercial liquid soap for your testing liquid. For your first test, use distilled water as a control. Put 25 mL of distilled water into a test tube and add one drop of liquid soap or detergent (the testing liquid). Shake for a few seconds.

Do you get suds that last for at least 10 seconds? If so, make a note that one drop of the testing liquid makes lasting suds in 25 mL of distilled water. If not, add a second drop of the testing liquid to the distilled water and shake again. Keep adding the testing liquid drop by drop until you get suds that last at least 10 seconds. Record the number of drops of testing liquid required.

Now test 25 mL of your permanent hard water in a test tube with the same procedure. Record the number of drops needed to make suds that last at least 10 seconds. Repeat the experiment with 25 mL of your temporary hard water. Record your findings again.

Try this procedure on other water samples. For example, see how your tap water at home and at school compares with distilled, permanent, and temporary hard water. Look for other water sources—rivers, lakes, and the ocean, for example—to test for hardness.

SOFTENING HARD WATER

A soap or detergent works better in soft water than it does in hard water. When soap is added to hard water, the soap first reacts with the calcium, magnesium, and/or iron salts in the hard water. The *product*—one of the substances formed—of this reaction is a grayish, scumlike material. Perhaps you noticed this scum during previous experiments. Only when all the calcium, magnesium, and iron salts are used up can the soap or detergent begin to make suds and to start cleaning.

Perhaps you can see why it is expensive to wash things in hard water. Some of the soap you use is wasted. The soap that reacts with calcium, magnesium, and iron salts cannot be used for cleaning. People whose tap water is hard often soften their water before using it to wash clothes or for bathing. Your next project is to learn how to soften water and to test some commercial water-softening products.

SAFETY NOTE
Wear safety goggles and a lab apron.

Add 25 mL of your permanent hard water to one test tube and 25 mL of your temporary hard water to a second test tube. Gently heat each test tube slowly until the water just starts to boil. Keep the water samples at the boiling point for a couple of minutes. Make a note of any visible changes in the test tubes.

Let the two samples cool. Then test each for hardness with the testing liquid according to the procedure used above. What effect, if any, did heating have on the hardness of the two samples? What, if anything, did you learn about the terms "permanent" and "temporary" hard water?

A number of chemicals can be used to soften hard water. You can test some of them. Put 25 mL of your permanent hard water in one test tube and 25 mL of your temporary hard water in a second test tube. To each test tube add 1 g of washing soda (sodium carbonate). Shake each test tube well. Now test the water in each container with the testing liquid according to the procedure described above. Decide how effectively, if at all, washing soda softens each type of hard water.

Washing soda is one of the simplest agents used for softening hard water. Two other softening agents you can make yourself are the following:

Agent 1: 1 g of washing soda mixed with 1 g of lime (calcium hydroxide)

Agent 2: 2 g of sodium metasilicate plus 2 g of sodium metaphosphate plus 1 g of trisodium phosphate

Make each of these two mixtures and find out how effectively 1 g of each softens a sample of your permanent hard water and of your temporary hard water.

Finally, a number of water softening products are commercially available. Ask friends, neighbors, and relatives to see what water softening products they use. Or purchase a sample of commercial water softeners at your local store. Find out how efficiently 1 g of each product softens (1) your permanent hard water and (2) your temporary hard water. Rank the commercial products from most effective to least effective. Devise a method for ranking the products on value as well, that is, on effectiveness *and* cost.

SOAP AND THE ENVIRONMENT

You probably have heard the term *biodegradable.* This means the ability of a substance to break down in natural conditions, for example, in water or soil. Until fairly recently, most detergents contained phosphates, which when released into the waterways contributed to the excessive growth of vegetation and subsequent destruction of fish habitats. Such detergents were not biodegradable; that is, they did not break down easily once they were released into the environment. Many states now regulate the amount of phosphate detergents may contain.

There are many projects to investigate in this area. Here are a few ideas:

• Are all soaps biodegradable? Are some more so than others?

• Investigating the above questions may lead you to ask: What does biodegradable really mean? Are there different degrees of biodegradability?

• Is biodegradable soap of the kind sold for backpacking trips, really better than conventional soaps and detergents?

4

PERSONAL-CARE PRODUCTS

For thousands of years, men and women have used chemicals to improve their appearance. We know, for example, that Egyptian women used an eye shadow made of malachite (an ore of copper) and an eyeliner that contained galena (an ore of lead). Women in colonial America used common garden products as beauty aids—for example, lavender, rose water, and cucumber cream as perfumes; beet juice as a lip coloring; and burnt cork as an eyelash darkener. Today, people spend billions of dollars on perfumes, hair sprays, face creams, toothpaste, and many other personal-care products.

In some cases, these products contribute to a person's health. Brushing with toothpaste or tooth powder, for example, does more than make your teeth bright and shiny. It also reduces the risk of tooth decay and gum disease. In other cases, the product is intended solely to make a person more attractive.

Most of the personal-care products you buy in a store (see Figure 10) are basically quite simple. They consist of

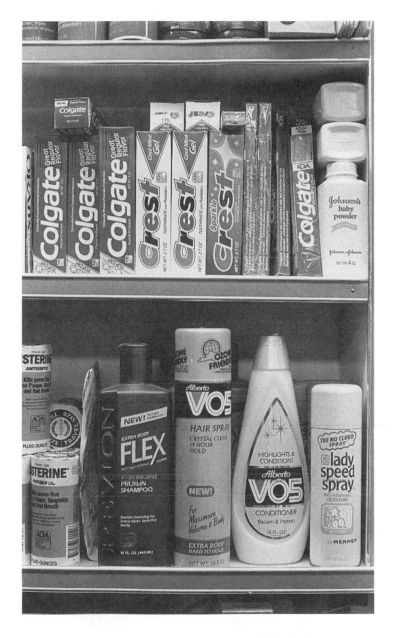

FIGURE 10. DO YOU USE ANY OF THESE
PERSONAL-CARE PRODUCTS?

two or three major ingredients. Different forms of a product have a variety of "extras" added to the basic formula. For example, various brands of cold cream all have the same basic ingredients. But they contain different perfumes, dyes, oils, and other substances in addition to the basic ingredients. In this chapter, you will learn how to make and test a number of personal-care products.

COLD CREAM

Cold cream is used to remove makeup and to keep skin clean and moist. It consists of two main substances: white beeswax and mineral oil.

SAFETY NOTES
1. Review the general safety precautions on pages 14–19.
2. Wear safety goggles and a lab apron.
3. Borax is slightly toxic.

To make your own cold cream, combine 50 g of beeswax and 250 mL of mineral oil in a large beaker. Set the beaker in a water bath. Look at Figure 11 (and in the appendix) to see how a water bath should be set up. Then heat the mixture just until the beeswax dissolves.

In a separate beaker, *carefully* add 100 mL of boiling water to 10 g of borax. Stir until the borax dissolves completely. Next, add very slowly the hot borax solution to the beeswax–mineral oil solution. Stir the mixture constantly while you are combining the two solutions.

As the mixture cools, it will become thicker. While it is still slightly warm, you may add a few drops of food coloring or a few drops of perfume. Transfer the warm cold cream to a beaker. When the cold cream is completely cold, try a few drops of it on the back of your hand.

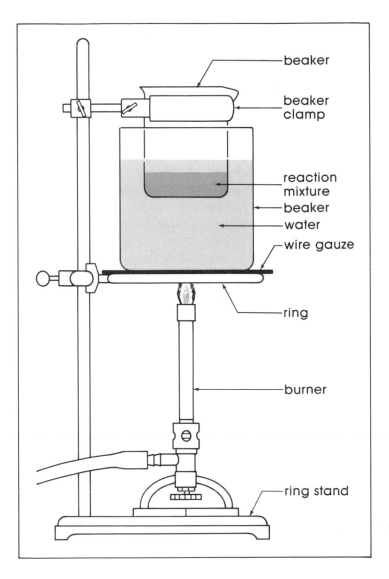

FIGURE 11. THE WATER BATH USED IN THE
COLD-CREAM PROJECT

Some people are sensitive to certain chemicals. Test only a small amount of cold cream at first. If your skin gets red or itchy, wash the cream off immediately and do not use it on your skin again. Also, tell your teacher if you have any problems. In any case, do not leave the cold cream on your hand for more than a few minutes. After that, wash your hands thoroughly with soap and water.

How can you test the quality of this cold cream? Invent a test that you can use on this homemade product and on commercial cold creams available at a local store.

You can change the cold cream you made in a number of ways. For example, you could increase or decrease the amount of beeswax or mineral oil in the basic formula. Try different proportions of these two materials and see how the quality of your cold cream is affected. Do not use any materials other than those mentioned above, however.

FACE CREAM

Another product whose composition is like that of cold cream is face cream. Why would a person use a face cream? Read the label on a container of a commercial face cream to see what its recommended uses are.

SAFETY NOTES
1. Review the general safety precautions on pages 14–19.
2. Wear safety goggles and a lab apron.
3. Stearic acid is slightly toxic.
4. Triethanolamine is flammable. Keep it away from flames.

The procedure for making face cream is like that for making cold cream. Combine 25 g each of stearic acid and mineral oil with 15 g of lanolin in a beaker. In a water bath, heat the mixture until everything is liquid. In a second beaker, add 20 drops (2 mL) of triethanolamine to 50 mL of water. Heat this mixture to boiling. Add the stearic acid–mineral oil–lanolin mixture to the water solution very slowly and with constant stirring. Stir until you have a smooth, creamy mixture. Allow to cool. How does this mixture compare with the cold cream you made?

How important are the proportions of stearic acid, mineral oil, and lanolin in the above formula? What would happen, for example, if you used 25 g of lanolin rather than 15 g? Try varying the quantities of each ingredient to see how they affect your final product. Do not use more than 20 drops of triethanolamine, however. You also could try leaving out one ingredient at a time. That way you can see how each ingredient affects the properties of the face cream.

LIPSTICK

Lipstick is a product whose primary purpose is to make a person more attractive. The wax and oil in the lipstick may also soften a person's lips. But the color that lipstick adds to a person's face is the main reason it is used.

SAFETY NOTE
    Wear safety goggles and a lab apron.

The method for making lipstick is similar to that for making cold cream and face cream. The ingredients are changed slightly to make a product that is firmer than the creams. Before making your lipstick, prepare a container in which to put it. Wrap a piece of heavy aluminum foil around a small test tube. Make sure the aluminum foil is pulled tightly around the test tube and that it has no holes in it. Slip the test tube out of the aluminum container. Now you have a holder for your lipstick.

In a beaker placed in a water bath, melt 50 g of white beeswax. Add slowly and with constant stirring 50 mL of mineral oil to the melted wax. You can add color to this mixture in one of two ways. First, you can add a few drops of food coloring to the liquid wax–mineral oil mixture. Or you can add some crushed crayon to the mixture. Be sure that the crayon you use is marked "nontoxic."

Continue heating until the color is evenly distributed through the mixture. Then pour the mixture into the aluminum foil container you made. Set the filled container into an ice bath. An ice bath is simply a large beaker filled with ice (see the appendix under "4. Water Baths"). Simply put the aluminum container in the middle of the ice in the ice bath. Then leave the ice bath in a refrigerator until the lipstick becomes solid.

Test your completed lipstick on the back of your hand. Use only a small amount of the product at first. Do not leave the lipstick on your skin for more than a few minutes. Then wash it off with soap and water. Wash it off immediately if you have a skin reaction. Compare the appearance and texture of your homemade product with those of a few commercial lipsticks. How is your lipstick better? How is it not as good as the commercial products?

Repeat the lipstick preparation with variations. For example, use a 50-50 mixture of white beeswax and spermaceti wax instead of pure beeswax. Or try another oil in place of mineral oil. Castor and sesame oils are two possibilities. How do these changes affect the properties of your final product? What other changes in the original formula might affect the lipstick you make? Try out some of your ideas.

TOOTH POWDER
AND TOOTHPASTE

Brushing your teeth is a good idea for many reasons. First, it removes and kills bacteria that cause tooth decay and gum disease. Second, it helps prevent bad breath caused by those same bacteria. Third, it makes your teeth clean and attractive.

Your tooth powder or toothpaste should have two properties. First, it should be mildly abrasive. It should be able to scour bacteria without damaging tooth enamel. Second, it should be slightly *basic*. The bacteria in your mouth prefer to live in an *acidic* environment, so a basic tooth powder or toothpaste will help to reduce the growth of bacteria. (If you aren't sure of the meanings of *acidic* and *basic*, check the glossary under *acid* and *base*, respectively.)

A tooth powder or toothpaste also may contain an ingredient such as powdered white soap that causes sudsing. A sudsing action helps stir up and wash away bacteria. Commercial tooth powders and toothpastes usually contain food coloring and something to add a pleasant flavor. These additives should not contain sugar, however, for reasons that you should be able to guess.

Tooth Powders

Tooth powders and toothpastes both have these general properties. The two products differ from each other only in the form in which they are made. One, of course, is a powder while the other is a cream. The simplest tooth powder you can make is a mixture of two parts baking soda and one part table salt. Make a mixture of this composition. Which compound provides the abrasive action? Which provides the sudsing action? Which makes the tooth powder basic? Try brushing your teeth with this tooth powder. What are its advantages and disadvantages?

The main ingredient in most commercial tooth powders is one of two materials: (1) precipitated chalk, a form of calcium carbonate or (2) pumice, a powdery form of volcanic rock. Prepare a combination of precipitated chalk (or pumice), powdered white soap, a flavoring, and a food coloring. Try various proportions of these ingredients until you get a combination that looks, smells, and feels attractive.

Ask your teacher if it is safe to taste your product. If it is, taste no more than a tiny amount, about the size of a pinhead.

Test the effectiveness of your tooth powder as a stain remover. Find a porcelain plate that you can stain with grape juice or some other colored material. Then find out how well your tooth powder removes the stain from the plate. Apply the tooth powder by moistening a toothbrush, making a paste of the tooth powder with the toothbrush, then scrubbing the plate with the pasty tooth powder.

Collect as many commercial tooth powders as you can. Think of a method for comparing these tooth powders as stain removers, then rate the tooth powders from best to poorest. Would the tooth powders rank in the same order as decay fighters? Also think of a method for testing this property of tooth powders.

Toothpastes

You can make a simple toothpaste by adding glycerin to precipitated chalk or pumice. Add the glycerin to the chalk or pumice a little at a time until you have a material with the consistency of toothpaste. Test your toothpaste for its ability to remove stains from a porcelain plate.

As you brush the plate with your toothpaste, observe (look, smell, and touch) its properties. What qualities does it lack that you think a toothpaste should have?

You can make your toothpaste more efficient and more pleasant by adding additional ingredients, for example, powdered white soap and flavoring. What proportion of chalk (or pumice), soap, glycerin, and flavoring produces the best toothpaste? You may taste a very small amount of the toothpaste provided that you are sure the ingredients are pure and you have your teacher's approval to do so.

MOUTHWASHES

A mouthwash won't keep your teeth clean, but it may kill some of the bacteria in your mouth that cause bad breath. At least that's what advertisers tell you. You can make your own mouthwash and test its ability to kill bacteria. You then can compare your homemade product with mouthwashes available in local stores.

SAFETY NOTES
1. Review the general safety precautions on pages 14–19.
2. Wear safety goggles and a lab apron.
3. Borax is slightly toxic.

A simple homemade mouthwash can be made by adding a pinch of zinc chloride, 5 g of borax, and 10 g of sodium bicarbonate to 250 mL of water. *Don't try to use this mouthwash,* but you can test its bacteria-killing properties. Here's how.

Sterilize two petri dishes and covers by heating them in a 200°C oven for 1 hour. Make a nutrient agar solution by combining equal quantities of nutrient agar powder and water. Boil the solution for 2 minutes. Pour enough agar solution into the petri dishes to make a layer about 0.5 cm deep. Cover the dishes and set them aside.

When the dishes are cool and the agar has become solid, remove the covers from both dishes for about 10 minutes. During this time, bacteria in the air can settle on the agar. Add enough of your homemade mouthwash to one dish to just barely cover the agar. Do nothing to the second dish.

Replace the covers on both dishes, tape them shut, and place them in a cool, dark place. Once a day for the next few days, check each dish for any changes. Do not open the dishes. You should be able to see bacteria growing on the untreated agar. What do they look like? Do you see bacteria growing on the agar treated with mouthwash? What can you say about the bacteria-killing properties of your mouthwash?

Ask your teacher how to dispose of the agar and properly clean the petri dishes and covers.

Now compare some commercial mouthwashes with your own. Collect or buy at your local store three or four kinds of mouthwash. Read the label on each product. What ingredients do the commercial mouthwashes contain that your homemade mouthwash does not? Try adding one or more of these missing ingredients to your own mouthwash. See how the addition of these ingredients affects the bacteria-killing properties of your mouthwash.

Find a way of measuring the effectiveness of each new mouthwash you invent. Finally, use this method to measure the bacteria-killing effectiveness of the commercial mouthwashes you found. Can you rate these mouthwashes from most effective to least effective as bacteria killers?

PERFUMES

The perfumes you buy today are made of either natural or synthetic materials. If a perfume contains natural odors, those odors come from flowers, leaves, fruits, nuts, berries, or other pleasant-smelling parts of plants. These pleasant-smelling compounds—called *essential oils*—do not dissolve in water, so they are extracted from a plant with a fat. The easiest and least expensive fat for you to use in this exercise is lard. Once you've removed the essential oils with lard, you'll dissolve those oils in *denatured alcohol* (see glossary). The alcohol–essential oil mixture is your homemade perfume.

SAFETY NOTES
1.   Review the general safety precautions on pages 14–19.
2.   Wear safety goggles and a lab apron.
3.   Both lard and denatured alcohol (see the glossary) are very flammable. Keep them away from flames.

Select a nonpoisonous plant material whose odor you especially like: rose petals, mint leaves, pine needles, eucalyptus bark, or lemon rind, for example. Chop the material into small pieces. The smaller the pieces, the more essential oil you'll be able to remove. You should have about 250 mL of plant material when you are done.

Add the plant material and 100 g of lard to a beaker. Be sure the lard is absolutely pure and clean. Set the jar in a water bath and heat the water until the lard begins to melt. Continue to warm the water to keep the lard liquid for about an hour. Add more water from time to time to maintain the same volume. At the end of an hour, essential oils in the plant material have dissolved in the lard.

Now add 30 mL of denatured alcohol to the jar. Mix the solution thoroughly. You want to be sure that the essential oils completely dissolve in the alcohol.

Finally, set up a distillation apparatus as instructed in the appendix. *Distillation* is a technique for separating the parts of a mixture. Have your teacher inspect the apparatus and supervise the distillation. Start the distillation by heating the water bath to boiling. At this temperature, the alcohol–essential oil mixture will vaporize inside the flask. As it rises and leaves the flask, the vapor will cool and condense. The condensed vapor—your homemade perfume—travels down the condenser and into the collection flask. Remember to be extremely careful when working with the mixture, since it is very flammable.

After examining the perfume, set it aside. Notice any changes that occur in its odor over a period of weeks and months. You can use this perfume in the cold cream, lipstick, soaps, and other products you made in this and other chapters.

Once you have mastered the technique described above, you can make other types of perfumes. Choose other plant materials with pleasant odors from which you would like to have a perfume. Repeat the above process with each of these materials, one at a time, until you have your own "line" of perfumes.

5

SOILS

Most people know something about growing plants. You may have a vegetable garden that supplies food for your dinner table. Or you may grow flowers for the beauty and pleasure they bring. Or your house may be filled with potted plants that bring a touch of nature into your daily life.

Whatever your contact with plants, you probably know something about the conditions they need to grow properly. For example, you know that plants need certain kinds of soil to grow in. They must also have the correct amounts of water and sunlight. In this chapter you will find out how some of these conditions affect plant growth.

SOIL COMPOSITION

How many different kinds of soil can you find within five blocks of your home? The materials that make up soil are usually described by one of four terms: clay, silt, sand, and humus. Materials made of very small particles are classified as *clay*. Those with slightly larger particles are called *silt*. Those with the largest particles are called *sand*. The following chart shows the generally accepted way of classifying these three kinds of materials:

Material	Particle Size
clay	less than 0.002 mm
silt	0.002 mm–0.02 mm
sand	0.02 mm–2 mm

Finally, materials formed by the decay of plants and other organic matter are called *humus*.

One way to begin your study of soils is to make a collection of these four basic materials.

SAFETY NOTES
   Keep your hands away from your face when handling soil. Wash your hands thoroughly when you are through handling the soil.

Obtain enough of each kind of soil to fill a 1-L container. You will use these materials for the experiments described later in this chapter.

Most soils are not pure clay, pure sand, or pure anything else. They are mixtures of the four basic components. The term *loam* is used for any soil that contains some combination of these basic materials.

In the following projects, you will want to compare not only the four pure types listed above, but also some examples of different kinds of loam. You can make up some soil samples of your own. For example, you might create one that contains 25% of each basic component, and another that contains 33% of clay, silt, and sand.

Also collect some samples of soil near your home or school. Try to get soil samples that are as different from each other as possible. Make and collect enough of each kind of soil to fill a one liter jar of each. Label your soil jars as follows: Jar A (clay); Jar B (silt); Jar C (sand); Jar D (humus); Jar E (one kind of homemade soil); Jar F (a second kind of homemade soil); Jar G (one kind of found soil); Jar H (a second kind of found soil); Jar I, Jar J, Jar K, etc. (other kinds of homemade and found soils).

PHYSICAL CHARACTERISTICS OF SOIL

Two of the physical characteristics that determine soil quality are (1) what fraction of each basic component is present in the soil, and (2) how well the soil holds water.

SAFETY NOTE
Wear safety goggles and a lab apron

Soil Composition

One way to distinguish soils is by the percentage of clay, silt, and sand they contain. The amount of each component can be determined by a settling test. To do this test you need a 100-mL graduated cylinder or some other tall glass cylinder. Do a test first with a soil whose composition you know.

Make a mixture consisting of one-third clay, one third silt, and one-third sand. Fill the cylinder halfway with this mixture. Add enough water to fill the cylinder to within 5 cm of the top. Put your hand over the top of the cylinder and shake it vigorously for about a minute. Place the cylinder someplace where it will not be disturbed.

After an hour, examine the mixture in the cylinder. Find the places at which the sand, silt, and clay have settled out. You should be able to see sand up about one third of the way, silt another third of the way up, and clay in another layer of the same depth.

Now repeat the settling tests with the found samples in Jars G, H, etc. Write down the percentage of clay, silt, and sand in each of these soils.

How will the presence of humus in these soils affect your results? Use the humus in Jar D to invent a variation of the settling test. See if you can determine the sand/silt/clay/humus composition of your sample soils.

Moisture Retention

Various soils retain moisture for different amounts of time. In some soils, water drains through rapidly. Other soils hold water for a long time. To determine moisture retention, you will need a large funnel and filter paper to fit the funnel. Refer to the appendix to learn how to fold and use a filter.

Place enough sand in the funnel to come within about 3 cm from the top of the filter paper. Support the funnel above a beaker that will hold at least 250 mL of water. Pour 250 mL of water over the sand in the funnel. After 5 minutes, measure the volume of water in the beaker below the funnel. Record the amount of water retained by the sand.

As you think about this experiment, or when you do it the first time, you will recognize that you will have to refine this procedure to get good results. Think of the additions or changes you need to make to get dependable results.

Repeat this procedure with samples from Jars B, C, D, E, F, G, etc. Compare the amount of moisture retained by each soil material (A–D) and each kind of soil.

Think about this question: Would your results be any different if you waited 10 minutes before measuring the amount of water in the beaker? If you waited 15 minutes? One hour? Twenty-four hours? Repeat your experiments, if necessary, to learn the answers to these questions. Think about any changes in the experimental design that may be necessary to keep your results dependable with longer waiting times.

How does water retention affect plant growth? Do

some kinds of soil hold water too long for plants to grow well? Do some kinds of soil lose water too fast? Think of a project that will allow you to answer these questions. Find out how plant growth is affected by the way various soils retain water.

SOIL ACIDITY

A farmer or gardener (see Figure 12) should know how acidic a soil is, since plants have different requirements. Some prefer acidic soils, while others do not.

FIGURE 12. TESTING SOIL ACIDITY IS IMPORTANT
FOR GARDENERS AND FARMERS ALIKE.

Suppose you accidentally spilled battery acid in your back yard. You would soon learn that no plant will grow in soil with this much acidity. You would make a similar discovery if you spilled household lye. In this case, the soil would be too basic. Plants will grow in soil with just the right acid-base balance.

Chemists express the acidity of a material with a number called the *pH.* The pH scale ranges from about 0 to about 14. A material with a high acidity has a low pH number. For example, battery acid has a pH of about 1. A basic material has a high pH number. A water solution of household lye, for example, has a pH close to 14.

Pure water is neither acidic or basic. Its pH is 7.0. Materials that are weak acids have a pH slightly less than 7.0. For example, shaving lotions contain weak acids that give them a pH of about 5.0. Weak bases have a pH slightly greater than 7.0. Most shampoos contain weak bases that give them a pH of about 8.0. Most plants grow in a soil that is neutral or slightly acidic. The table shows the pH of some common solutions:

pH OF SOME COMMON SOLUTIONS

13   lye

12   washing soda

11   household ammonia

10   milk of magnesia

9   seawater; baking soda

8   bile;
     blood

7   pure water;
     milk

6   normal rain water

5   black coffee

4   tomato juice

3   apple juice; soft drinks;
     vinegar; lemon juice

2   gastric juices

1   battery acid

Chemists use an *indicator* to determine the pH of a material. Indicators are chemicals that are one color at one pH and a different color at another pH. You will find indicator paper very useful in much of your research. Ask for a few pieces of universal indicator paper from your teacher. Have the teacher show you how to use the paper.

You also can purchase a soil testing kit at any garden supply store. A soil testing kit contains, among other things, an indicator solution. You use the indicator solution differently from the way you use indicator paper. Read the directions on the kit to find out how to use the solution.

SAFETY NOTES
1. Review the general safety precautions on pages 14–19.
2. Wear safety goggles and a lab apron.

To test soil acidity, place about 5 g of the soil from Jar E in a large test tube. Add enough water to nearly fill the test tube. Shake the test tube vigorously for about 1 minute. Take a drop of water from the test tube and place it on the indicator paper. Compare the color on the paper with the chart on the indicator package.

Alternatively, test the soil sample with the indicator solution from the soil testing kit according to directions on the package. What is the pH of the soil from Jar E?

• Repeat this test with soils from the remaining jars (F, G, H, I, J, etc.). Make a list of these soils from most acidic to least acidic. Include the approximate pH of each soil. Various types of plants prefer soils with different acidities. Find out what kinds of plants would grow best in each of the soils you have collected.

• Most soils are acidic because humus contains organic acids produced during decay. Some plants grow well in acidic soil. Other plants prefer soil that is less acidic. Design a project to find out what kind of soil various plants prefer. Select as many different kinds of plants as possible. You may want to ask a nursery person for some suggestions. But do not let the nursery person tell you which plants prefer which soils. Then there would be no point in doing this project.

• Suppose your soil is too acidic for plants to grow in. You can reduce the soil's acidity by adding lime (calcium hydroxide), a weak base. Here's how to test the effects of adding lime to soil.

Make a solution of limewater by adding about 1 g of slaked lime (calcium oxide) or powdered lime (calcium hydroxide) to 100 mL of water. Shake the mixture well and filter the resulting solution. The filtrate, your limewater test solution, should be kept in a stoppered bottle. It will not last more than 24 hours. You will have to make a fresh solution each day you work on this experiment.

Select the soil samples you found to be most acidic (that had the lowest pH). As before, add 5 g of each of these soils to a separate test tube. Add water to each test tube and shake well for about a minute. Drop a short piece of indicator paper in the test tube.

Then add limewater, drop by drop, to each test tube. Shake the test tubes briefly after each drop, and notice the color of the indicator paper. Find out how many drops of limewater are needed to make each soil neutral (pH = 7.0).

Figure out a way to give a numerical value to the acidity of these soils. For example, if your most acidic soil is 100, how can you express the acidity of the next most acidic soil?

• Soils are sometimes too basic. Find out how you can make a soil more acidic. Then use that method to increase the acidity of your soil samples. Invent a method, like the one described above, with limewater to measure how much you can increase the acidity of soils.

SOIL NUTRIENTS

Farmers and gardeners need to know the nutrient value of their soil to be successful at their endeavors.

Plants consist primarily of carbon, hydrogen, and oxygen, elements they get easily from air, water, and soil. But plants also need three other nutrients in relatively large amounts: nitrogen, phosphorus, and potassium. These *macronutrients* may also be available in air, water, and soil, but sometimes not in the quantity that plants need to grow properly. Finally, plants also require small amounts of other elements such as calcium, copper, iron, magnesium, and chlorine. These *micronutrients* may or may not be present in soil in the amounts needed by plants.

In some cases, they occur in too high a concentration and may cause damage to plants.

Farmers and gardeners may want to test for the presence of macronutrients and micronutrients in their soils. If these nutrients are lacking, they can be added in the form of fertilizers.

A number of companies manufacture soil-testing kits. These can be used, under supervision, for testing soil for both macronutrients and micronutrients. The following tests, for phosphorus and iron, can be done without a kit.

Testing for Phosphorus

Phosphorus usually occurs in soil in the form of phosphate. You can try the phosphate test first with a known compound, sodium phosphate. Dissolve 1 g of sodium phosphate in 100 mL of water in a test tube and add 2 drops of dilute nitric acid. To 5 mL of this solution, ask your teacher to add an equal volume of ammonium molybdate solution. Heat this mixture nearly to boiling in a water bath, stirring from time to time. *Do not boil.* The appearance of a yellow precipitate indicates the presence of phosphorus in the form of phosphate.

To test for phosphate in soil, prepare each soil sample by mixing 5 mg of the sample with 100 mL of water. Shake the mixture vigorously for about 1 minute and filter. Test 5 mL of the filtrate from each soil solution with 5 mL of ammonium molybdate, as you did with the sodium phosphate. Make a list of the soils in which you were able to detect phosphorus in the form of phosphate.

Testing for Iron

Note: The iron test described on page 36 also can be used to test for iron in soil. Write your own experimental directions for testing for iron in your soil samples.

HYDROPONICS

The practice of growing plants without soil is called hydroponics (see Figure 13). In hydroponics, the nutrients that

FIGURE 13. A COMMERCIAL HYDROPONICS FACILITY.
ARE ANY VEGETABLES IN YOUR LOCAL
SUPERMARKET GROWN IN SUCH A FACILITY?

plants need are dissolved in water. Plants are held in place in clean sand or gravel, and the nutrient solution washes through the sand or gravel and over the plant roots.

Learning about hydroponics can be an interesting and ambitious project. One problem is finding out what chemicals work best in the water solution. Another problem is determining the correct concentration of the nutrient solutions. A third problem is finding out how long the solution needs to remain in contact with the plant roots. Yet a fourth question is what difference, if any, the supporting medium (sand, gravel, etc.) makes on plant growth.

If you are interested in learning more about hydroponics, design a series of experiments that will allow you to test each of these factors, one at a time.

6

FIBERS AND DYES

People who lived in the Middle Ages made their clothes out of wool, cotton, linen, silk, and other natural fibers. These fibers come from plants (the cotton and flax plants; see Figure 14) and from animals (sheep and silkworms). People today wear clothes made from these same natural fibers and from dozens of synthetic fibers produced as the result of chemical research. In this chapter, you will investigate some of the properties of natural and synthetic fibers. You also will learn how to add color (to dye) those fibers.

NATURAL AND SYNTHETIC FIBERS

To do these projects, you will need pieces of cloth made of wool, cotton, linen, silk, nylon, polyester, and any other synthetic fiber you can find. Each piece should be about 30 cm square.

FIGURE 14. COTTON PLANTS (TOP) AND COARSE
THREAD MADE FROM COTTON

Preparing the
Cloth Samples

To prepare the cloth samples, boil each fabric for about 5 minutes in a solution of 25 g of washing soda (sodium carbonate) in 1 L of water. This step cleans the cloth and removes any sizing on them. *Sizing* is a material added to cloth to fill the pores in its fibers.

Dry the cloths completely and cut each one into a square about 6 cm on a side. Find a way to label each square so that you will always know what fiber it is made of.

Appearance and Strength
of the Fibers

From a square of each natural fabric (wool, cotton, linen, and silk), pull out a single fiber. With a magnifying glass or microscope, examine the structure of the individual fiber. Make a sketch of what you see and compare the structures of the four natural fibers. How do the plant fibers differ from the animal fibers, if at all?

Repeat this process with a single fiber of nylon, polyester, and all other synthetic fibers you have collected. How do the synthetic fibers differ from each other? How do they differ from natural fibers, if at all?

One desirable characteristic of a fiber is its strength. Which of the fibers you have collected is the strongest? Which breaks most easily? Invent a method for determining the strength of each of your fiber samples. Make a list of your fibers, arranged from strongest to weakest.

Before you start the next set of projects, think about this question: Suppose you wanted to invent a new kind of fiber that could be used to make clothing. What properties should that fiber have? Make a list of properties you think are important. Then compare that list with the properties you actually test in the next few exercises. Based on your list, you may want to add some additional tests to those that follow.

Absorption and Shrinkage

Knowing what happens to a fiber when it gets wet is important. The first property to study is how much water a fiber absorbs (soaks up) when it gets wet. At the same time you can determine how much a fiber shrinks when it gets wet and dries out.

Find the weight of one square of each of your fibers. Write down these weights. Then place one sample of each fiber in a liter beaker and completely cover the samples with cold water. Allow the fibers to sit in the water for 15 minutes.

Pour off the water and place each fiber square on a dry piece of wood for 5 minutes. Finally, weigh each sample and record its weight when soaked with water.

Now you have the weight of each sample, dry and wet. You can calculate the percentage of water absorbed by each fiber with the following formula:

$$\frac{\text{% of water}}{\text{absorbed}} = \frac{\text{weight of sample wet} - \text{weight of sample dry}}{\text{weight of sample dry}} \times 100\%$$

Rank your sample fibers from the one holding the most water to the one holding the least water. What practical value is the property of water retention in the manufacture of clothing? In the manufacture of fibers for other uses?

Now repeat this procedure with hot (90°C) water. Is the amount of water retained by your fabric samples different when the water is hot compared to when it is cold? What is the practical value, if any, of this finding?

Shrinkage is another important property of fabrics. Why? The exercises outlined above provide you with one way of finding out how much various fibers will shrink in cold and hot water. Think about the changes or additions you would have to make in these exercises to determine shrinkage. Then carry out the necessary experiments. Rank your fibers in order, from the one that shrinks the least to the one that shrinks the most. Is your list the same for cold water as it is for hot water?

Some fabrics are advertised as water-repellent or waterproof. These fabrics are coated with a material that prevents water from soaking into the material. Obtain two or three samples of such fabrics. Design a project that will test the ability of these fabrics to repel water. Find out how much better they are in repelling water than are other fabrics.

Acids, Bases, and Bleach

When people get hot, they perspire. Perspiration is a slightly acidic solution. What effect will slightly acidic perspiration have on cotton, wool, nylon, and other fibers?

Some washing materials (such as soap) are slightly basic. What is likely to happen to cotton, wool, nylon, and other fabrics when they are exposed to a basic solution?

Finally, people often like to bleach their clothes when they wash them. How does bleach affect various types of fabric?

SAFETY NOTES
1. Review the general safety precautions on pages 14–19.
2. Wear safety goggles and a lab apron.
3. Vinegar, ammonia, and bleach all have strong, unpleasant odors. Avoid smelling these chemicals. Do the projects in this section under a fume hood if your classroom has one, or in a well-ventilated room.
4. Do not mix ammonia and bleach; toxic fumes will result.

To test the behavior of your fiber in an acidic solution, mix one part of household vinegar with two parts of water. Soak each cloth sample in this acidic solution for 30 minutes. Remove, rinse, and dry the fabric, and examine the sample.

How has each fiber changed, if at all? In what ways would you guess the fibers *might* change? How can you test for each possible change you can think of? Devise a method for each test, carry out the test, and compare all fibers on each particular property.

You can test the effect of a basic solution on fibers with a weak solution of household ammonia. Mix one part of household ammonia with two parts of water. *Use caution,* as the ammonia has a strong, offensive odor. Repeat the tests you invented for the acidic solution with this basic solution.

Are your fibers affected by the basic solution in the same way they were by the acidic solution? What differences, if any, do you find?

You can use commercial household bleach for your final set of tests. The purpose of these tests is not to look for color changes but to see how the bleach affects the fibers themselves. Will the bleach destroy some fibers? Will it weaken some? Will it have any other kinds of effects on the fibers?

Soak one square of each fiber in bleach for 15 minutes. Then rinse each square thoroughly and dry it completely. Examine the fibers under a magnifying glass or a microscope. Do the bleached fibers look any different from the unbleached ones? Invent a test that will show whether the fibers have been weakened. Make a list of fibers on which bleach should not be used.

Combustibility
Manufacturers need to know which fibers will burn and, if they do, how they burn.

To test a fabric's combustibility, hold a very small sample square of fabric with a pair of tongs, forceps, or tweezers. *Very carefully* bring the square into contact with the flame of a Bunsen or alcohol burner turned to a low setting.

Notice whether the square chars (gets black without burning) or actually burns and if either occurs, how soon. Also notice any odors associated with the charring or burning. Review page 14 on the correct method of testing for odors. Repeat this test with your other fabric samples. Also include in your tests materials that are labeled "fire-retardant" or "fire-resistant." Write a brief statement for each sample that describes the combustibility of the fabric.

Bacterial Action

Everyone knows that many fabrics just "wear out." Shirts develop holes and frayed edges for no reason other than they get old—or so it seems. But one reason fabrics (and other materials) "wear out" is that bacteria attack fibers. The bacteria digest chemicals in fibers, weakening and destroying those fibers, and causing fabrics to come apart.

Are some fibers more resistant to bacterial action than others? Do some resist decay entirely? The following project is one way of answering those questions.

Place a sample square of each fiber in the bottom of a liter beaker. Cover the cloths with dirt to the top of the container. Dirt is a good source of the kind of bacteria that cause decay in nature. Almost any source from which you take your dirt will provide you with an adequate supply of bacteria.

Set the beaker aside in a dark, warm place for at least a month. Make sure that the dirt stays moist—not soggy, just damp. Warm, dark, moist conditions are the best environment for bacteria to live in.

At the end of a month, uncover the fabric samples, wash them carefully, and allow them to dry. Notice whether there are any observable changes *before* you clean and dry the cloths. Then compare each fabric *after* cleaning and drying with a new piece of the same fabric. Examine each pair with a magnifying glass or microscope to see if you can find any visible changes.

Of course, there may be changes that are difficult to see even with a magnifying glass. How could you modify this project to detect other changes such as these?

Also, one month beneath dirt may not be the correct exposure time. Would you see changes after one week? After three months? How could you change this project to see how "time exposed to bacteria" affects fabric decay?

Prepare a list of fabrics that seem somewhat resistant to decay and a list of those that do decay. What practical applications, if any, can you see for the results of this project?

Heat Retention

People wear clothes for many reasons. One of the most important is to stay warm. Are some fibers better than others at keeping a person warm? If so, which fibers are they? Be sure to include in your test fabrics such as down, pile, polyester, and polypropylene as well as other fabrics listed above.

Write your own instructions for this project. What you need to find out is how easily heat passes through each of the fibers you have collected. Those that hold heat in well might be good for winter clothing. As a result of your investigations, list those fibers that retain heat best and a list of those that lose heat most rapidly.

Another way of retaining heat is by layering cloth. Two or more pieces are sewed together to make a garment. Does the air trapped between the layers retain heat? Find out the best way to layer fabrics to improve heat retention.

You can also test the effects of moisture on heat reduction. Do all fabrics keep you warm whether they are wet or dry? Or do some fabrics lose their ability to retain heat when they get wet? Which fabrics are better at retaining heat when they are wet? Design one or more projects to answer these questions.

DYES

At one time, most of the clothes people wore were white, gray, black, or brown. The reason was that those are the natural colors of wool, cotton, linen, animal skins, and other materials from which clothes were made.

People did know how to color with plant roots, leaves, bark, flowers, and other natural products. But these coloring materials—*dyes*—were often too expensive for ordinary people to use. A shade of purple once came to be known as "royal" purple because it was so expensive to make that only kings and other members of the royalty could afford to have their clothes dyed to that color.

Today that situation has changed. Chemists have invented dozens of synthetic dyes that can be made inexpensively. Now almost anyone can wear a shirt dyed to royal purple, or any other brilliant color.

Cloth can be dyed in many different ways. Sometimes you simply put the cloth and the dye into a pot of water (or some other liquid), and the dye sticks to the cloth. Remove the dyed material, wash and dry it, and you have a colored fabric. A dye that behaves this way is a *direct dye*. Other kinds of dye require additional steps in order to attach the colored material to the cloth.

The question that always has to be asked about dyeing is how long the fabric will keep its color. Perhaps you have had a T-shirt that began to fade after only one or two washings. After a dozen washings, it might have reverted to its natural, undyed color.

A dyed material that keeps its color after many washings is said to be *colorfast.* In the following projects, you should always test your dyed materials to see if they are colorfast. Here's how to do that.

After the cloth has been dyed, allow it to dry completely. Then wash the dyed cloth in warm, soapy water, as you would wash a shirt at home. See if the cloth loses any of its color. Sometimes it's hard to tell if any of the dye has washed out. It may help to look at the wash water. What would that tell you?

If you are imaginative, you may be able to invent a method for measuring *how much* dye is lost after each washing. Then you can arrange your dyed cloths in order from most colorfast to least colorfast.

Direct Dyeing

Malachite green is a direct dye. You can color some fabrics simply by combining the dye and the fabric in solution. Here's how to dye with malachite green.

SAFETY NOTE
    Wear safety goggles and a lab apron.

Dissolve 0.1 g of the dye in 200 mL of water. Heat the solution to boiling while stirring. Place one square of each fabric you want to test (cotton, wool, silk, nylon, etc.) in a test tube. Cover the square with the hot dye solution for 5 minutes. At the end of 5 minutes, remove the square from the test tube and test it for colorfastness. Make a record of the fibers that are dyed with malachite green by this method.

Listed below are a number of other common dyes.

Find out which of these, if any, are also direct dyes and, if so, with which fabrics they can be used. In addition to the dyes listed, ask your science teacher about other dyes to test. Finally, test one or more commercial dyes to see if they are direct and, if so, on what fabrics. Can you tell from the directions on the dye packet if it is direct or not?

Common dyes: alizarin, blue indigo, congo red, fuchsin, logwood, methyl orange, para red.

Vat Dyeing

A vat dye is one that does not dissolve in water, so it can't be applied by direct dying. Instead, the dye is chemically changed to a soluble form in a reaction vessel (the "vat"), the cloth is added to the vat, then the dye is chemically changed back to its original form. During the process, the soluble form of the dye attaches to the cloth. When it is converted to its original form, the dye regains its color while attached to the cloth.

SAFETY NOTES
1. Review the general safety precautions on pages 14–19.
2. Wear safety goggles and a lab apron.
3. Sodium hydrosulfite is an irritant and is toxic. If you spill any on yourself, wash it off with soap and water.
4. Sodium hydroxide, whether solid or in solution, is caustic and toxic and is an irritant. It will burn your skin and dissolve clothing. If you spill any on yourself, wash it off immediately with soap and water.

Try vat dyeing using blue indigo powder. Ask your teacher to do the following steps: Place 0.2 g of the dye, 0.2 g of sodium hydrosulfite, 1 g of sodium hydroxide, and

20 mL of water in a 250-mL flask. Stopper the flask and shake it well for about 3 minutes. Dilute this solution to 100 mL.

Soak the first fabric sample in this solution for about a minute. Remove the sample and hang it from a clothesline for about 5 minutes. Repeat the process with each of the other fabric samples. Which fabrics can be dyed by this method?

At the conclusion of this section, you should have a fabric-dyeing guide. The guide will tell you which fabrics can be dyed with each dye by each of the two methods you learned about.

7

DRUGS AND MEDICINES

One of the most important contributions that chemists have made to modern life is the development of drugs and medicines. For almost any physical disorder you can think of—from a stomachache to cancer—medication is available.

Most of these products are too complicated for you to make or analyze. But some drugs and medicines are fairly simple chemicals. You should be able to work with them with simple equipment in your own laboratory.

ANTACIDS

Antacids are a very popular over-the-counter (OTC) product, as you can see from the display shown in Figure 15. An OTC product is one that can be purchased without a prescription. An antacid is used to treat an upset stomach, heartburn, or other discomfort of the digestive system.

These conditions develop when the stomach releases too much hydrochloric acid. The acid causes a burning

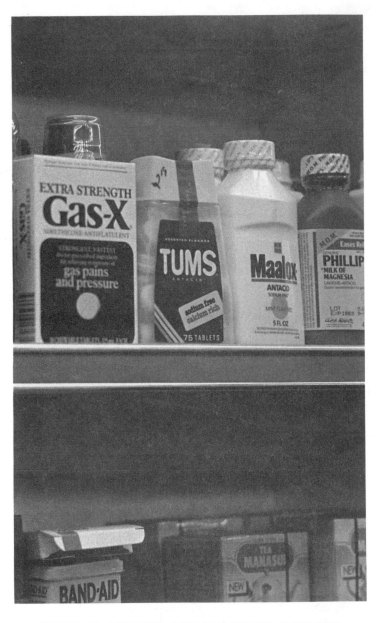

FIGURE 15. ANTACIDS ARE PART OF THE AMERICAN
WAY OF LIFE, AS ARE STRESS AND OVEREATING.

sensation, the release of gas, and a general discomfort. Antacids are chemicals that react with the excess hydrochloric acid, thus reducing these unpleasant effects.

Neutralizing Stomach
Acid with a Base

You can easily demonstrate these bodily processes in a test tube.

SAFETY NOTES
1. Review the general safety precautions on pages 14–19.
2. Wear safety goggles and a lab apron.
3. Hydrochloric acid is corrosive and toxic and an irritant. Use caution in working with it. If you spill any on yourself, wash it off immediately with soap and water.
4. Sodium hydroxide is caustic and toxic and an irritant. It will burn your skin and dissolve clothing. If you spill any on yourself, wash it off immediately with soap and water.

Combine 5 mL of dilute hydrochloric acid and 10 mL of water in a flask. Measure out the hydrochloric acid as accurately as you can. This solution represents the contents of a human stomach (although not precisely so).

Add 3 drops of phenolphthalein solution to the flask. Phenolphthalein is an indicator, a substance that is one color in one pH range and a second color in a second pH range. (Look back at pages 70–71 to review the pH scale). You will see that phenolphthalein is colorless in an acid solution. In a basic solution, the phenolphthalein turns pink.

To the acid solution in the flask, *cautiously* add a 10% solution of sodium hydroxide, a little at a time. The reaction that takes place in the flask is similar to the one that takes place in your stomach when you take an antacid.

The best way to add the sodium hydroxide is with a medicine dropper. Swirl the flask as you add the sodium hydroxide. Notice that the solution turns pink at the point the sodium hydroxide hits the acid solution, but that the pink goes away as the sodium hydroxide reacts with the acid.

You are looking for the point at which all the acid is exactly neutralized by (has reacted with) the sodium hydroxide. You will know you are near that point when the pink color lasts a little longer with each addition of sodium hydroxide. As you near this end point, begin adding the sodium hydroxide one drop at a time. Add a drop, swirl the flask, and see if the pink color lasts for 10 seconds. If the color fades within that time, add another drop, swirl, and watch again.

Eventually, a single drop of sodium hydroxide will make the solution in the flask turn pink "permanently," that is, for at least 10 seconds. When this happens, you will know that all the acid has been neutralized by the sodium hydroxide.

Practice really does make perfect here. The more often you repeat this process, the better you will get at knowing *exactly* when you have reached the end point, exactly when all the acid has been neutralized. So you may want to do a half-dozen trial runs with sodium hydroxide before going on to the next section.

Note: Your teacher may show you how to do titrations, as described in the appendix. Titration is the most precise method for doing this kind of experiment.

Testing Antacids

You can use this procedure to study the effects of antacids. By measuring the amount of sodium hydroxide you added in the above procedure, you can tell how much of this chemical was needed to neutralize your sample of stomach acid. Now you can repeat the process with commercial antacids and see how they compare as acid neutralizers.

The antacids you buy in a store do not contain sodium hydroxide, but they do contain other compounds that are chemically similar to sodium hydroxide. Collect as many commercial antacids as you can. Read the label on each to see what the "active ingredient" is. You should see names such as aluminum hydroxide, calcium carbonate, magnesium hydroxide, and sodium citrate. For purposes of comparison, you should also test a common home remedy for stomach distress, baking soda (sodium bicarbonate).

SAFETY NOTES
1. Review the general safety precautions on pages 14–19.
2. Wear safety goggles and a lab apron.
3. Hydrochloric acid is corrosive and toxic and an irritant. Use caution in working with it. If you spill any on yourself, wash it off immediately with soap and water.

The procedure for testing antacids is like the one described for sodium hydroxide. First, combine 5 mL of very dilute hydrochloric acid, 10 mL of water, and 3 drops of indicator in a flask. Remember to measure the 5 mL of acid as accurately as you can. In this part of the project, you should use a different indicator, such as bromophenol blue. Bromophenol blue is yellow when the pH is less than 3.0 and purple when the pH is more than 4.6.

Choose a liquid antacid, such as milk of magnesia, for your first test. Add the antacid a little at a time, as you did with the sodium hydroxide. Keep track of the exact amount of antacid you add. Precision in your measurements is very important in comparing these products. Use titration equipment for this project if you have learned how.

As you approach the end point, add antacid a drop at a time until you get a permanent (lasting at least 10 seconds) color change. Record as precisely as possible the amount of antacid added. You may want to run a second and third trial to be sure your results are correct.

Repeat this process with other liquid antacids you have collected. Make sure that you begin each time with exactly the same amount of hydrochloric acid. Do at least three trials with each antacid to be sure your results are accurate. Make a chart that compares the amount of antacid needed to neutralize your sample of stomach acid. Which product is most effective?

Finally, test the solid antacids (including baking soda) that you have collected. You will have to modify the above procedure, of course, since you can't add a solid to the acid solution with a medicine dropper. You should be able to find a method, however, for comparing the acid-neutralizing properties of your solid antacids. To be of greatest value, this method should allow you to compare *all* antacids, solids and liquids, with each other.

The final product of this project should be a list that ranks acid-neutralizing efficiency of the antacids you studied. You also may want to see how cost is involved in this comparison. Invent a method for calculating the "acid neutralizing effectiveness per penny" for each product studied.

APPENDIX
SPECIAL PROCEDURES IN CHEMISTRY

Over the centuries, chemists have developed many specialized techniques for working with materials. This appendix explains a few of those techniques. The following explanations are not intended to be complete. Ask your science teacher to demonstrate any of the techniques you need to use in your chemistry projects.

1. Distillation
Distillation is a way of separating solids, liquids, and gases from each other. Place the mixture to be separated in the distilling flask, as shown in Figure 16. Add one to two boiling stones to the flask. Connect the tube at the lower end of the condenser to a water outlet. The tube from the upper end of the condenser should empty into the sink. Start the water flowing through the condenser. Place a collecting flask under the open end at the bottom of the condenser.

The various components of the mixture boil at different temperatures. As each component boils, it turns into a

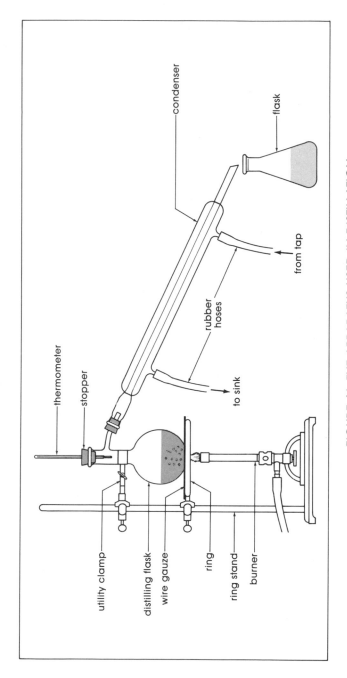

FIGURE 16. THE APPARATUS USED IN DISTILLATION

vapor, rises in the flask, and enters the condenser. Water running through the outer jacket of the condenser cools the vapor and changes it back into a liquid. The liquid is then captured in the receiving vessel. Solids are left behind in the flask.

The thermometer in the distilling flask shows the temperature at which each component boils off. When a particular component has boiled away, the temperature rises. At that point, you should place a new receiving flask under the condenser outlet to capture the next component.

2. Filtration

The easiest way to separate a solid from a liquid is by means of filtration. Fold a circle of filter paper and insert it into a funnel, as shown in Figure 17. Carefully pour the solid/liquid mixture into the filter paper. The solid remains on the filter paper while the liquid (filtrate) passes through into the beaker below. In situations where filtration takes place very slowly, special kinds of filtration systems are available. The Büchner funnel shown in Figure 18 is an example.

3. Titration

Titration is a method for determining precisely how much of a liquid is used in an experiment. Ask your teacher to demonstrate the proper method for doing a titration. The following is a general introduction to that procedure.

The long glass tubes in Figure 19 are burettes. They are calibrated in tenths of a milliliter. Before using a burette, wash it thoroughly with soap and water. Rinse it with water two or three times, then with a small amount of the solution to be used in the burette. Fill each burette with one of the solutions to be used in the titration. Label each burette so that you know which solution it contains.

Place a flask under one burette. Release a precisely known amount of solution from this burette by carefully turning the stopcock. Add an indicator to the solution in the flask. Place the flask under the second burette.

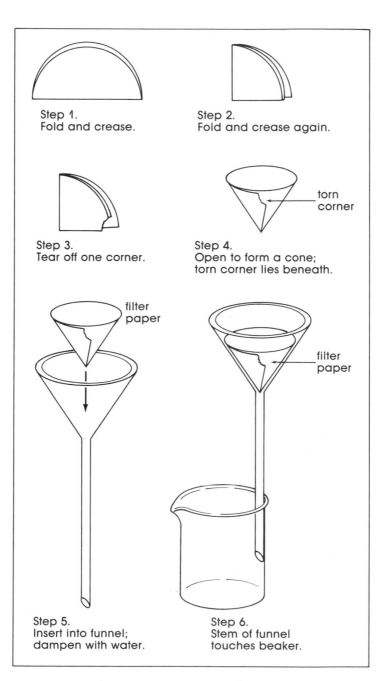

FIGURE 17. THE PROPER METHOD FOR FOLDING AND USING FILTER PAPER

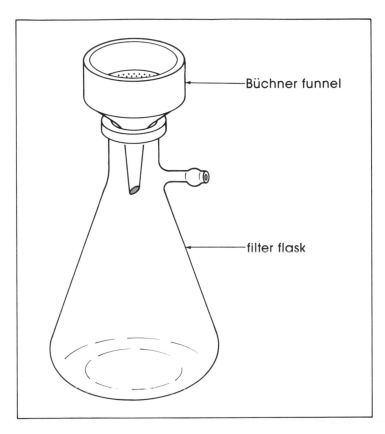

FIGURE 18. A BÜCHNER FUNNEL

Allow the second solution to run into the flask slowly. Swirl the flask as the second solution is being added. At exactly the point where the first solution is used up (has reacted with the second solution) the indicator changes color. Watch carefully for this change of color. It will tell you when exactly equal amounts of Solution 1 and Solution 2 have reacted in the flask. This will allow you to calculate how much of Solution 1 is equivalent to how much of Solution 2. Remember that titration is an exact procedure, so you need to be especially careful to keep all of your equipment very clean.

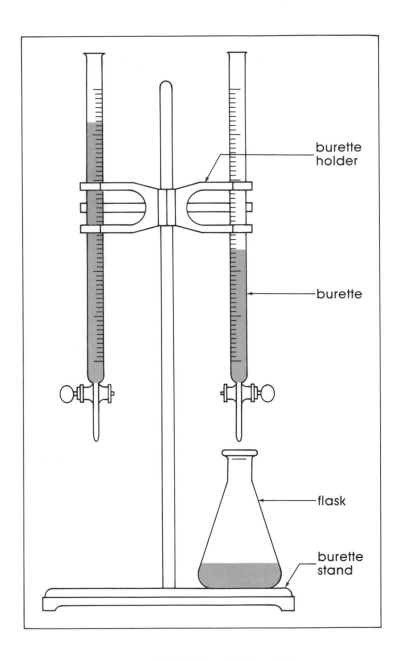

burette
holder

burette

flask

burette
stand

**FIGURE 19. A PAIR OF BURETTES
USED FOR TITRATION**

4. Water Baths

Some liquids are flammable. If you tried to heat them with an open flame, they might catch fire. Another way to heat such liquids is in a water bath, like the one in Figure 20.

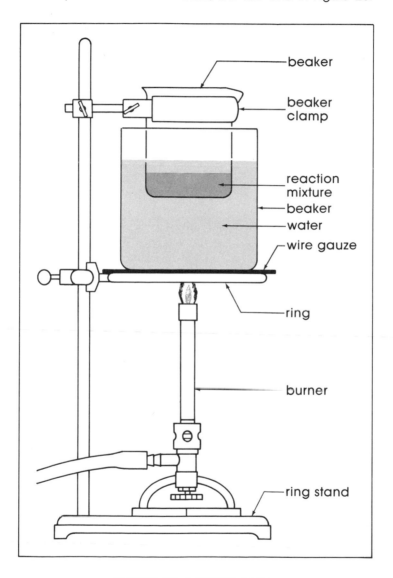

FIGURE 20. A WATER BATH

You heat a beaker of water with a flame to whatever temperature is required, turn off the flame, then place the beaker that contains the chemical(s) to be heated into the hot water. The hot water heats the reaction beaker. You may need to continue heating the water to keep it at the correct temperature. The double boiler system used by cooks is an example of a water bath.

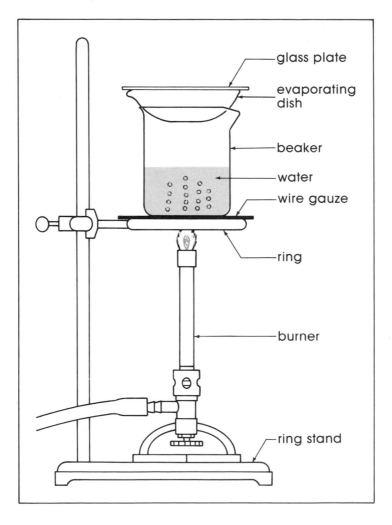

FIGURE 21. A STEAM BATH

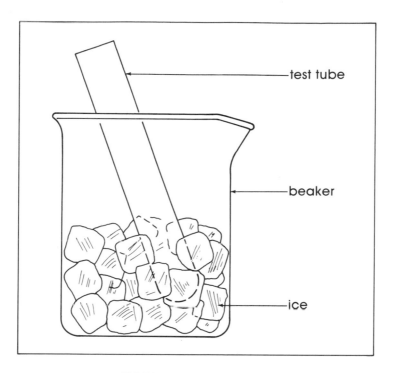

FIGURE 22. AN ICE BATH

A water bath can be converted to a steam bath. In a steam bath, you place the reaction container above boiling water, as shown in Figure 21. Steam from the boiling water heats the reaction container.

Finally, a similar setup can be used for cooling containers. An ice bath like the one in Figure 22 consists of a large beaker filled with ice, rather than with water. You place the test tube containing the chemical(s) to be cooled on top of the ice. The ice then cools the chemical(s) in the test tube.

GLOSSARY

Following are some common chemical terms that occur in this book. To look up any term not defined here, see the glossary in any introductory high school or college chemistry textbook.

acid (acidic). A substance that contains a high concentration of hydrogen ions. The acidity of a substance is measured on the pH scale. Acids have pH numbers that range from 0 up to 7. An acid is the chemical opposite of a base. Lemon juice, battery acid, and vinegar are common acids. A substance with the properties of an acid is said to be acidic.

base (basic). A substance that contains a low concentration of hydrogen ions and a high concentration of hydroxide ions. Bases have pH values that range from 7 to 14. A base is the chemical opposite of an acid. Household ammonia, milk of magnesia, and lye are common bases. A substance with the properties of a base is said to be basic.

denatured alcohol. Ethyl alcohol (ethanol) to which some foreign substance has been added. The alcohol is treated in this way so that it cannot be used for drinking purposes. Many kinds of denatured alcohol are available. *Denatured alcohols are toxic and should not be swallowed under any circumstances.* They are also flammable and must be kept away from open flames.

distillation. A technique for separating solids, liquids, and gases in a mixture (usually two or more liquids) from one another. See the appendix.

filtrate. The liquid that passes through a filter paper during the process of filtration.

filtration. The process by which a solid is separated from a liquid. See the appendix.

indicator. A dye that is one color in one kind of solution and a second color in a different kind of solution. The most common indicators are those used to distinguish between an acidic and a basic solution, or between solutions with different pH values. For example, the indicator methyl red is red at a pH less than 4.8 and yellow at a pH greater than 6.0. Phenolphthalein is colorless at a pH less than 8.2 and pink at a pH greater than 10.0.

pH. A number used to measure the acidity and alkalinity of a substance. The pH scale ranges from about 0 to about 14. Acidic substances have low pH values. Basic substances have high pH values.

precipitate. The solid formed within a solution usually as the result of a chemical reaction.

product. One of the substances produced in a chemical reaction.

BIBLIOGRAPHY

Many laboratory manuals written for high school and college chemistry courses describe experiments like the ones in this book. In many cases, the manuals provide more detailed instructions and call for more sophisticated equipment. They are usually good guides, however, for the person who wants to go beyond the information provided in this book.

Manuals in organic chemistry are often useful because most topics in this book fall within that field of chemistry. Ask a high school or college chemistry instructor for specific recommendations.

Following is a list of some especially good manuals:

Bolton, Ruth P., Elizabeth V. Lamphere, Mario Menesini, and Paul C. Huang. *Laboratory Activities in Action Chemistry.* New York: Holt, Rinehart, and Winston, 1979. A laboratory manual for a chemistry course designed for students who are normally not very interested in science.

Jones, Mark M., John T. Netterville, David O. Johnston, and James L. Wood. *Laboratory Manual for Chemistry, Man and Society,* 2d ed. Philadelphia: Saunders, 1976. Designed for college students, these experiments are fairly advanced, with good ideas for "going further."

Korchin, Florence G. *Science in the Marketplace,* 3d ed. Red Bank, N.J.: Tiger Publications, 1987. A wonderful combination text and laboratory manual that deals with many aspects of common materials. Includes information and experiments in mathematics, biology, and physics, as well as chemistry.

Saland, Leonard. *Practical Chemistry Labs.* Portland, Maine: J. Weston Walch, 1989. Sixty simple experiments on chemical techniques, chemical principles, and common materials.

Scott, Lawrence W., John W. Hill, Leon M. Zaborowski, and Peter Muto. *Chemical Investigations for Changing Times,* 4th ed. Minneapolis: Burgess, 1984. A laboratory manual for a college chemistry textbook on chemistry of everyday topics.

Summerlin, Lee R. *Chemistry of Common Substances.* Morristown, N.J.: Silver Burdett, 1979. Very simple, but very interesting experiments with many common materials.

A number of trade books also contain some good suggestions for chemical experimentation with familiar materials. Among these are the following:

Beeler, Nelson F., and Franklyn M. Branley. *Experiments in Chemistry.* New York: Crowell, 1952. An old book, but one of the best ever written on this topic. Highly recommended.

Cobb, Vicki. *Chemically Active.* New York: Lippincott, 1985. Some interesting experiments in chemistry.

————. *The Secret Life of Cosmetics.* New York: Lippincott, 1985. Experiments with and information about soaps, lotions, creams, perfumes, makeup, hair products, and other personal care products.

Stone, A. Harris. *The Chemistry of a Lemon.* Englewood Cliffs, N.J.: Prentice-Hall, 1966. A host of experiments that involve the use of lemons in cleaning silver, removing rust, making fire extinguishers, etc.

Tocci, Salvatore. *Chemistry with Everyday Products: Experiments and Projects in Consumer Chemistry.* New York: Arco, 1985. Some excellent ideas for chemistry projects with everyday products.

A number of good books are available on the general topic of how to select, design, and carry out research projects in science.

Beller, Joel. *So You Want to Do a Science Project.* New York: Arco, 1982.

Tocci, Salvatore. *How to Do a Science Fair Project.* New York: Watts, 1986.

Van Deman, Barry A., and Ed McDonald. *Nuts and Bolts: A Matter of Fact Guide to Science Fair Projects.* Harwood Heights, Ill.: The Science Man Press, 1982.

Here are several titles on laboratory safety:

Chemical Risk: A Primer. Washington, D.C.: American Chemical Society, 1985. Write: ACS, 1155 16th Street NW, Washington, D.C. 20036. Free.

Council of State Science Supervisors. *School Science Laboratories: A Guide to Some Hazardous Substances.* Washington, D.C.: U.S. Consumer Product Safety Commission, 1984. Write: Council of State Science Supervisors, Route 2, Box 1449, Lancaster, VA 22503. $5.75.

Division of Training and Manpower Development. *Manual of Safety and Health Hazards in the School Science Laboratory.* Cincinnati, Ohio: U.S. Department of Health and Human Services, 1980.

Flinn Chemical Catalog Reference Manual. Batavia, Ill.: Flinn
  Scientific, 1983. Write: Flinn: P.O. Box 231, 917 West Wilson Street, Batavia, IL 60510. Free.
Gerlovich, Jack, and Gary E. Downs. *Better Science Through Safety.* Ames, Iowa: Iowa State University Press, 1981.
Manning, Pat and Alan R. Newman. "Safety Isn't Always First,"
  School Library Journal, October 1986.
Norback, Craig T. (ed.). *Hazardous Chemicals on File.* New
  York: Facts on File, 1988.
Weiss, G. (ed.). *Hazardous Chemicals Data Book.* 2nd ed.
  Park Ridge, N.J.: Noyes Data Corporation, 1986.

Finally, you probably will be interested in and find very useful two other resources. One is the monthly magazine *Consumer Reports.* The magazine does regular reports on consumer products that, although more sophisticated than the ones in this book, may give you good ideas about techniques and other research to pursue.

Also, two invaluable "recipe books" for all kinds of chemicals that you can make and use in your own home are:

Stark, Norman. *The Formula Book.* Kansas City: Sheed Andrews and McKeel, 1976.
———. *The Formula Manual,* 3d ed. Cedarburg, Wis.: Stark
  Research Corporation, 1975.

INDEX